SUCCESS:

FULL THINKING

Tapping into the Unlimited Resources of Mind

by

Friar Justin Belitz, OFM

Pen & Publish

Co-published by The Franciscan Hermitage and Pen & Publish, Inc.
The Franciscan Hermitage
3650 E. 46th Street
Indianapolis, Indiana 46205 USA
www.FrJustin-Hermitage.org

Pen & Publish, Inc.
Info@PenandPublish.com
www.PenandPublish.com
(812) 837-9226 or (866) 326-7768

Printed in the United States of America

Cover lotus painting by Jeanette Larson.
Photograph courtesy of Garry Chilluffo (www.Chilluffo.com).

ISBN 13: 978-0-9779530-8-0
ISBN 0-9779530-8-4

ACKNOWLEDGEMENTS

My sincere thanks to Friar Mario DiCicco, OFM, who first introduced me to the Silva Mind Development class in 1974. That weekend changed my life forever!!!

My thanks also to the Silva family in Laredo, TX, who trained me in the knowledge and skills of meditation but who also gave me the opportunity to lecture internationally.

Lillian Kraeszig has been a volunteer for many years! Words cannot express my thanks for the time, expertise and patience she and Teena Weisman put into the important task of proofreading.

LuLu Kinnett, Chris Rathbun and Friar Bertin Miller, OFM, have been my supports on the Hermitage Board of Directors, especially when the challenges were great!

Finally, my gratitude to Claude Homann-Herimberg, who first invited me to Switzerland, and Marietta Kovacs, who continues my work in the French-speaking countries of Europe; Renée Bennett who first organized my work in Australia for many years; Nigel Taylor who continued to support my work in Perth; and Wendy Gellard of Peace Be Still, who presently coordinates my programs in Australia; Ann Irvine who coordinates my work in Lincoln, NE, Josephine Garretson who is my associate in Omaha, NE; Pat Kerlin of Katy, TX; Mary Fleece of Houston, TX, and so many others who have invited me to teach. This volume would not have been possible without the support of these and so many others. God bless you all!!!

Success:Full Thinking

The Franciscan Hermitage

The Hermitage is a healing center founded in 1984 in the belief that at times all of us need assistance in discovering and pursuing knowledge of our uniqueness and of our deeper selves. Participating in programs of The Hermitage expands awareness of oneself as both teacher and learner. It provides an atmosphere of freedom for people to get in touch with the divine dimension of their humanity and tap into it for the creativity necessary to serve our times.

Visit www.FrJustin-Hermitage.org
for additional information and products.

Contact Fr. Justin Belitz at FrJustinBelitz@hotmail.com
for classes, speaking engagements, interviews and appointments.

Contact info@PenandPublish.com
for volume purchases and publishing to serve your mission.

Fr. Justin Belitz
Photograph by Tom Subject

CONTENTS

FOREWORD

Mind over matter.

The power of positive thinking.

You can be anything you want to be.

You can do anything you set your mind to.

How often have you heard those old maxims? Probably since you were a youngster. How often have you ignored them? Probably since you were a youngster. Well, ignore them no more; they are not just banal sentiments. Fr. Justin Belitz will prove it to you in this wonderful little book. Your mind, he says, is a great gift, our connection with the Divine. It has unlimited potential. And he shows you simply and clearly how to make it work for you.

Oh no, you say, not another self-help book! No it's not just another self-help book. This book is based on years of study and practice. Years of experience through lecturing and teaching that Fr. Justin has done around the world. Feedback and support from the many-thousands of people who have tried it on for size and found that it works.

How do you get control of your mind and make it work for you?

Read on and let Fr. Justin show you. Let him show you how to use your mind to its full potential to be a better person physically, mentally and spiritually. He promises that if you use the information in this book to develop habits of thinking creatively you will have a life full of love, peace, health, happiness and other good things, and that you will be in touch with all that is good, true and beautiful.

Not a bad deal, coming from a man of God.

Thomas Jansing
Journalist - Rome, Italy

PREFACE

The greatest resource we have as human beings is the mind. It is our connection with a Power that has no limit! That means you and I have access to a universal energy we can use to "see" into the future, solve problems of any kind in the present, and put us in touch with all that is good, true and beautiful!!!

Jesus, Buddha, all the saints and holy people of the past everywhere on the earth learned to tap into the unlimited power of Mind and demonstrated its power. Jesus, for example, said: "The Kingdom of God is here at hand, it is within!" Then he added: "Do you see the works I do? Greater than these shall you do!!!" – The Buddha went in search of Truth, but did not find it until he sat quietly under a tree and turning his attention inward, discovered the Truth in the experience of Mind. From that moment on, he spent his life helping others to come in touch with this inner Power. – St. Francis got direction for his life as he sat quietly in the chapel of San Damiano. There in the quiet, he heard the voice of Jesus telling him: "Francis, go rebuild my Church for as you see it is falling into ruin!" - Joan of Arc listened in the quiet to the voices that gave her direction. -- Always, the information came through the experience we call "mind." It is our connection with the Divine!!!

The purpose of this volume is to help you, the reader, become aware of the power of mind, to which you are eternally connected AND understand the simple tools that anyone can use to direct this unlimited Power toward peace and love. If you believe that you and God are one, you can open the door to Universal Intelligence and connect with Cosmic Energy! With this connection, you can join the army of believers who, together, will make our world a peaceful and loving place – a heaven on this earth.

I

THE REAL YOU

The purpose of this chapter is to clarify some basic ideas that relate directly to YOU. For example, when we talk about you as "matter" we can talk about your body and point to your eyes, ears, arms, etc. It is not difficult to discuss the material side of your person.

However, when we try to talk about the "non-matter" side of you, we immediately run into difficulty. For example, how can you talk about a "thought?" You may know what I mean when I use the word "thought" because you have had the experience of a thought. But how can you "picture" a thought?

Actually, "thoughts" and other aspects of "spirit," cannot be expressed *adequately* in words because they don't have limits; nor are they made of parts. It is difficult to talk about any part of our lives that is "non-matter."

We have the same problem with words like mind, self, God, soul, life, etc. All of these terms point to the "non-material world." We are connected to this "non-material" world and experience it every day, but we have a difficult time thinking about "non-matter" and even more difficulty talking about it.

As human beings all of us are composed of matter and spirit, body and soul. This dual reality is something from which we cannot separate ourselves – it is part and parcel of who we are.

On the one hand, matter consists of objects made of parts. Everything we experience, the chairs we sit on, the clothing we wear, our homes, flowers, animals, etc. – all are made of parts. We don't have much difficulty thinking about or imaging anything in this "material" dimension.

On the other hand, in the world of spirit, there are no parts. Spirit is "one." We speak, for example, about God as being "one." But as human beings, we cannot imagine anything that is simply "one" – something that has no parts.

We have the same difficulty when we try to talk about ideas like "love" or "energy." St. Paul, for example, spoke of God as "love." But we cannot "picture" love the way we picture a car or a house. "Love" by its very nature is inexpressible.

Consider parents who hold a new-born child for the first time. That experience is life-transforming! It is as if past and future implode into a moment that is "eternal." Such an experience is so wonderful that the parents would like it to go on forever! But as powerful as this experience may be, it can never be expressed *adequately* in language. By its very nature, this kind of experience is *inexpressible*.

Trying to discuss any "spirit" reality is challenging. To use another example, we cannot picture "Universal Intelligence" or "Cosmic Energy." We can *understand* what these terms mean but there is no way we can express their full reality in language that is *adequate*. These realities can be *experienced* but they simply cannot be expressed *completely*, because by their very nature, they are *inexpressible*.

At the outset, therefore, it is important, even essential, for the reader to understand this principle: **We cannot adequately express anything in the spirit world.** This is a constant and fundamental challenge for all of us when trying to discuss anything about the world of "spirit."

So how are we going to talk about "spirit"? Traditionally, all human beings on the planet have resorted to the use of signs, *symbol*s, comparisons, metaphors, story telling, etc. For example, we use the sign of a heart as a symbol of love, and most everyone can "read" this sign and understand it. The heart, in this case, is only a "sign" pointing to a spiritual reality we know and experience as "love."

The same is true of the idea of God. We cannot "picture" God because God has no parts and is infinite. However, we can use a comparison. Using the concept of "energy," for example, we know energy is everywhere, in material objects, in outer space, in every human being and in every part of the universe. A comparison like this can help us understand and discuss "God" with such words as "cosmic energy."

As we move into a study of "thinking," which is "spirit," it will be helpful to have some definitions for words that relate to "spirit." This chapter may be challenging, but understanding of it is essential in order to understand the chapters that follow.

1. Self

Perhaps the greatest challenge of life is dealing with the idea of "self." By "self" I mean "that" which makes you the unique being you are. It is something essentially "spiritual" or "non-material"; it is not something you can touch, or measure, or describe. However, it is something you *experience* every day and something we all know to be real.

Trying to define "self" is like trying to define "room." When asked to describe a room, we usually begin by talking about what is in the room (e.g. the furniture that occupies the space, or the walls that define the space, or decorations that beautify the space). But all of those are incidental to the room. Only space is essential.

In much the same way, we describe our "selves" by talking about our bodies. "I am 5 feet, 9½ inches tall and weigh 150 pounds." These statements are not a description of "self," but rather statements about my body that defines the space in which I experience "self."

Sometimes we describe "self" by talking about what we do: "I am a lawyer," "I am a mother," "I am a student," "I am an athlete." These statements, however, do not define "self," either; they are rather descriptions of how the "self" functions or what the "self" does.

"Self" is "that" in each of us which we call "spirit" or "non-matter." It is the essence of who we are – some "thing" at the core of us that is always there – a thread of sameness that continues, even though externals change, somewhat like the space of a room that seems to change when we experience it with furniture and accessories, and when we experience it without furniture and accessories.

Recently, I heard a speaker trying to explain "self." He asked the audience to pay attention to the thoughts constantly going through their heads. Then he said, "You will find 'self' in the space between the thoughts."

According to the dictionary, "spirit" is "an animating or vital *principle* held to give life to physical organisms." In this definition, the term "principle" represents an *idea*, which is something we cannot draw or picture because it is "spiritual," that is, "not material." At the same time, the definition describes what the principle *does*, not what it *is*. As a result, the definition does not really tell us what "spirit" is – at best it gives us only a vague notion.

It is always a challenge for human beings to discuss "non–matter" of any kind using words. "Soul," for example, is a *theological* word that points to the non-material "self." "Intellect" and "will" are *philosophical* terms that point to the same "self." "Mind" is a *scientific* term pointing to the same "self." In each of these cases, the difficulty is the same: how can we name and/or understand a reality that is "non-matter" or "spirit?"

2. Mind

For our purposes here, it is valuable to have some idea about "self" as "mind." First of all, "mind" is not "brain." The brain is definitely physical, something we can see and touch. It is the organ directly below the cranium. "Mind," on the other hand, is entirely "spiritual" or "non-matter." It is not something we can see or touch, but something we *experience*.

Second, the mind can be seen as "energy" that works through and in cooperation with the "brain." "Mind," so to speak, externalizes itself through the "brain."

In a previous volume, "Success: Full Living," we compared "mind" with electricity and "brain" with a light bulb. Electricity, focused and working through the light bulb, produces light. Similarly, the "mind" focuses and works through the "brain" to produce knowledge and/or awareness.

Third, scientists have made some intellectual distinctions to help us better understand the "mind." For example, they talk about the conscious, the unconscious and the super-conscious mind. Because "mind" is spiritual, it is "one" and cannot be made of parts. The terms "conscious," "unconscious" and "super-conscious" are not three parts of "mind." They are rather terms to describe our *experience* of "mind."

"Conscious mind" can be described as our normal waking state. In this state, we can directly call to mind information and experiences used in daily functioning. For example, we can easily and quickly call to mind names of individuals with whom we live and work, remember how to pour water in a glass when we are thirsty, and recall the alphabet when looking up a telephone number, etc.

When we experience "mind" as "conscious," we can direct our attention to the beauty of a blue sky, the English assignment for tomorrow's class, or the task of cutting the grass.

"Unconscious mind" refers to our ability to hold information that *was* conscious at some previous time, but which cannot be recalled at present and which is being used automatically, without conscious attention.

Suppose you want to recall a phone number that you knew and used as a child, but which you cannot immediately call to mind. You know the information is "in your 'mind' computer," but you just cannot pull it out at this time. Then as you talk about old times and move from one memory to another, all of a sudden the number pops into your awareness. This kind of experience has led scientists to create the category "unconscious" or "subconscious."

Our experience of habits can also be explained by using the idea of "unconscious." When learning a language, for example, we learn one word at a time or one phrase at a time. As we repeat these words and word patterns over and over, they become so automatic that they begin to come out of our mouths "without thinking." This kind of automatic information processing is described as taking place in the "unconscious mind."

In the past, some authors used only these two classifications of mind; others used different terminology. Jose Silva, for example, spoke of "outer consciousness" and "inner consciousness." Shunryu Suzuki used the designations "small mind" and "big mind."

Besides these two kinds of mind experience, a third category, "super-conscious," was created more recently to explain the ability of "self" to access *all knowledge*: past, present and future.

"Super-conscious" is used, for example, to explain the human creative experience. Creativity is the process of producing a thought that has never been expressed before *and* which is not in the past experience of the individual (therefore not part of the "unconscious"). For example, when Beethoven wrote his Fifth Symphony he produced something that had never existed before. Einstein came up with the Theory of Relativity which neither he nor anyone else had thought of previously. Edison also pulled out of the "super-conscious" not only one invention after another, but also solutions to problems related to those inventions. These are all examples of the use of "super-conscious mind."

The wonderful fact about "super-conscious" is that all of us can tap into it every day, and we do - for example, when we solve a problem that is uniquely our own; like planning a party, composing a letter, or creating a meal.

The important idea here is that "mind" is a word that points to a *spiritual* reality – something that exists but does not have parts. The distinctions we make ("conscious," "unconscious" and "super-conscious") are purely intellectual, used merely to explain our *experience*. They do *not* refer to "mind" as having three parts. 'Mind" is "one." It is our *experience* of "mind" that is multiple.

This analysis might be compared to the distinction we make when we describe the experience of a ballet. We make distinctions between the music, the dance and the dancer, but our experience is *one* - only in the "mind" do we create distinctions among the three.

Or to use another comparison: Space is "one", even though we create walls to "divide" it, for example - into individual rooms in a house or building. The space may *seem* to be divided, but as soon as the walls are removed, we experience again that space is "one."

In much the same way, we talk about "mind" as being a *part* of the "self" when in fact the *reality* is "one." We can *imagine* the human "mind" as contained within the physical limits of the human body, but when the body is removed, e.g. in death, "mind" does not disappear – it is simply "one" again with "universal mind."

3. *God*

"Universal Mind" is a *scientific* term for what theologians call "God." The reality of "God" is also "spiritual," i.e. without parts, and so can be identified as "self." Here we have a profound spiritual truth that carries with it inherent problems.

All religions teach that God is present within every human being. Because the "self" and "God" are both "spiritual," they are "somehow" "one." God is "the supreme reality" with whom we are all united in one ultimate reality.

Jesus tried to explain this truth when he said, "I and the Father are one," and "I am the vine you are the branches." He was trying to get us to understand our oneness with "spirit," by using an analogy.

Even Jesus had the problem of limited means (language) to describe "unlimited reality" (God, Spirit, Self, etc.). No human being can *adequately* express this reality. We try, of course, but it is impossible to use language to describe something that is limitless!

Some traditional approaches use language that implies a separation between God and all creation. God is seen as being "in heaven" while all creation is "on earth." Such expression is still common and for a good many people quite adequate.

Others use a completely different approach. Earlier cultures, for example, spoke of the 'Sun God' or the 'Earth Spirit.' These terms were not used to identify the sun or the earth as a "god." Rather they were used to point to the Divine as *expressed* in the sun or the earth.

Please note that all of the above approaches are attempting to express "spirit." Historically, one group criticized the others, calling their expressions "heresy," because the words were not the same as their own. The fact of the matter is, no one statement is *adequate*, but each made sense in its own culture and expressed the reality from a different point of view.

The fact remains, no matter how we perceive God – the cause that is not caused, or the reality that is (always was and always will be), or the reality that sustains all reality – we will never be able to fully understand "God" (or "Mind," or "Self," or "Spirit"); nor will we be able to adequately express a reality that is simply "one."

Given all of the above, we can say that "mind" is like "God," in that both are "non-material," both simple, both unable to be fully understood and since we are each "mind" and "mind" is "one," we somehow must be one with "God."

4. *Spirit*

Every day we deal with two different aspects of *human* experience – "matter" and "spirit." The world of "matter" is tremendously diverse; it includes inanimate matter, plants, animals and human beings. This world is also one of excessive abundance: infinite space, countless heavenly bodies, endless varieties of plants and animals, deserts, seas, mountains, valleys, etc. It is in this dimension of "matter" that we experience pairs of opposites: day and night, summer and winter, male and female, birth and death. We feel more comfortable with this area of reality because our bodies are involved: we touch it, feel it, smell it, taste it and hear it. We find it easier to know, and to deal with, the material world.

"Spirit," on the other hand, is more challenging for the average human being, mainly because most of us do not spend time thinking or talking about it and because it is a world of total unity. In the "spirit world" there are no parts, no pairs of opposites, no abundance. As a result, the bodily senses become inadequate. What creates a still greater challenge is that we use the language of "matter" to try discussing "spirit" reality. Even though the world of "spirit" is without parts and totally one, we create intellectual distinctions which make it seem as though "spirit" is made up of parts. We create pairs of opposites: mind and emotions in "self," intelligence and instinct in "mind," love and fear in "emotions," etc.

When dealing with the spirit world, however, there are no diverse realities. There is only one reality; no parts, only oneness; no diversity, only unity. Making distinctions in the world of "spirit" is like distinguishing waves in the ocean. We talk as if each wave has a reality in and of itself, but a wave is nothing but an ocean "bump." A wave cannot separate itself from the ocean, it *is* the ocean. – Or to use another comparison, we talk about the "dance" and the "dancer," but in reality, the dancer *is* the dance! They are one and the same.

Notice the problem we have with the theological idea of "soul" or the scientific idea "life principle." We know there is individual and separate life in every cell of the body, but when we speak of a multitude of cells that form an organ (skin, for example) we talk as if there is still another principle *in the tissue* made up of skin cells. Then, when we put the organs together and speak of the body, we speak as if there is another principle (i.e. "soul") which animates the "person." Because it is impossible for "spirit" to be in parts, we must understand that life in the cell is the same life in the organ, and the same life in the person. Being logical, we could continue the pattern and say that life in one human being is the same as life in the whole of the human race, and the same in all life forms of the universe. In other words, there is only one "life principle," one "soul," one "God," one "mind." But because we are human beings living in the limits of time and space, we really cannot *fully* understand such utter simplicity or oneness.

Suppose, you understand that all life is "one" and that all living things are merely an expression of the same "life principle" but each in its own time and space. With this understanding you can also realize that one "life expression" has an effect on every other "life expression." The whole world of living beings can then be seen as "one."

Let me use an illustration. Imagine a skin cell in your hand. It is born, lives and multiplies in the same area; its *personal* experience is very limited even though it is connected to the "one" "life principle." Now, picture this cell making a judgment from its limited experience and saying to another skin cell: "Someone was trying to tell me that we are part of a large entity called a body, and this body has organs called liver, heart, kidney, etc. Isn't that stupid? Everyone here experiences that there are only skin cells. What foolishness!!!"

That kind of judgment, in my opinion, is as valid as an American saying that the American way of life is the only real and valid one; or a Roman Catholic saying that Roman Catholicism has all the truth; or married people saying their approach to relationship is the only valid one, etc...

The point I want to make here is this - spiritual reality is "one", but it can have many (even infinite) expressions.

One of the purposes of this book is to help you become more comfortable with and knowledgeable about "spirit" so you can develop the skills needed to deal with this reality more effectively.

What I believe we all must do is become aware of the reality of "spirit," *where we are all "one."* Only then can we hope to develop respect for one another and celebrate *the unity of experience, which we call "love."*

5. Experience

What seems so ironic is that even though we cannot *conceptualize* "spirit reality" using words like "mind" or "self" or "love," we *can* *experience* spirit.

Recall what can be described as a "significant" or "mystical" experience: falling in love for the first time. When you think of the person you love, you experience something very profound. You actually get into a state that you would like to be in forever. You would like past and future to stop so that you could remain in this euphoric state always. Such a profound moment seems to make time stop and nothing else seems to matter. Emotional experiences like these change our lives forever. The challenge is this: how can you get another person to fully understand what you feel. Words simply cannot do the job!!! To have an *experience* of "love" (as described above) is an *emotional* way of "knowing."

Knowing in a purely *intellectual* way is a completely different kind of "knowing." For example, pay attention to how you know "love" when you read the definition: "Love is an act of the will, whereby a person accepts another exactly as he/she is."

In both of these experiences (emotional and intellectual) we "know" something about "love" but each experience is very different.

The same difference can be observed when we know "beauty." For example, recall or imagine standing on a beach. It is a beautiful summer evening and you are alone watching the sun set into the sea. You go into a state of quiet in which "beauty" takes over your entire person. You fill with a great peace and seem to "go" to a completely different "place of knowing." - Such an emotional experience will carry you beyond physical reality to a "spirit reality" where you somehow become "one" with "beauty."

On the other hand, when you go to a dictionary, you "know" beauty from a purely intellectual "place." Beauty is "the quality or aggregate of qualities in a person or thing that gives pleasure to the senses or pleasurably exalts the mind of spirit." This kind of knowing is much different from the emotional *experience* of "beauty."

Both ways of knowing are valid but they certainly are different!

We all have experiences of being one with the "spirit reality." For example, this morning I relaxed and began to recall some of my earliest childhood memories; kneeling on the living room couch with my Mom when I was just 4 years old, peering through the window and waving good-bye to my older brother as he walked to kindergarten; my first day of school when I was 5; the smell of sawdust in my grandmother's grocery store when I was about 10; kissing my Dad at the breakfast table before he went to work; the excitement of getting a malted milk from Goodrich Dairy as a special treat; eating crackers and milk as an evening snack, etc.... As I recall these events, it is as if my "self" were looking at those scenes from the outside in. Yet, in reality, they are experiences produced from the inside out. I am unable to define "self," but I know this "self" is the same in all these past events. My *experience* tells me that the "I" I am now, is that same "I" in all my past experience. That "I" is one but in many different times and circumstances.

It is possible to validate "mind" in much the same way. I can recall diagramming sentences in grade school, working algebra problems in high school, struggling with philosophical concepts in college and the excitement of creating papers and discovering new ideas in graduate school. In all of this "mind" practice, something has always been the same, a thread that helps me know that my "mind" exists, and that all the mind experiences of the past are somehow happening in one "mind" – my "mind." No one has to prove to me that "mind" is "one." My own personal *experience* is my proof and I don't need any other proof. For me, "mind" is a reality because I know it firsthand.

So it is with realities of "God" and "spirit" – ideas that cannot be explained fully or expressed adequately, but which are clearly part of my experience.

My point here is that, in *your* life too, there are many aspects of life which you validate by your *experience*; important realities like "love," "peace" and "joy." In fact, one of the most important means of creating the thread of continuity in your life *is* experience.

I believe that all human beings must value individual experience, take what understanding we can from each experience, and make our individual ways into the future.

6. Conclusion

Because of the problems inherent in our human limitations, we can at most offer theoretical explanations of "mind" in relation to brain and body realizing that what we do is hopelessly inadequate. On the other hand, working with comparisons of many kinds, using stories, and referring to personal experience, we can gain *some* understanding, even though it be limited and incomplete.

As you deal with these ideas in this book, you will come to know more about yourself, especially that side of you that is not material. You are unique, a one-of-a-kind creation, a valuable person. But at the same time, you have a spiritual connection with all reality that makes you one with all creation. My hope is that as you work with the ideas presented in this chapter and work on the following exercises, you will come to know more about your "self" and be able to apply this knowledge toward living a full life!

7. Suggested Activities for Chapter I

1. Get into a quiet space, lie down, close your eyes and let your mind take you back to some early childhood memories. Get in touch with your "self" from the past and pay attention to the oneness of your "self" in the present.

2. Go for a walk in a park or in the country and pay attention to the sounds around you, the rhythm of your steps, the sensations in your body and the scenes around you. Pay attention to your "mind" as it moves from one perception to another.

3. See what you can do about paying attention to the experiences of the day. Simply reflect on the fact that "I am driving," "I am typing," "I am thinking," "I am working," "I am eating," "I am angry," etc. Experience your "self" as "I."

4. Read this chapter again and pay special attention to the examples. Create examples of your own.

II

THEORIES

Because the very nature of "non-matter" (Mind, Soul, God, etc.) is difficult to discuss, it is understandable that we will have difficulty also comprehending how "matter" and "non-matter" work together.

In this chapter we will discuss several theories that *try* to explain how mind and body, working together, create human experience.

Before we begin, however, I want to remind you that any author (whether they be a scientist or theologian) will admit that it is impossible to explain *everything*. Always keep in mind the principle: **We cannot adequately express anything in the spirit world.** For that reason, scientists and theologians create "theories" that give *some* idea of how the world functions BUT they will be the first to admit that no one theory "tells it all."

1. Brain/Mind Theory

This theory is dualistic, that is, it points to two worlds of reality; one "material," the other "non-material" (spiritual). The brain is the physical "machine" and the mind is the "energy" that makes the machine work. A workable analogy might be a light bulb (corresponding to the brain) and electricity (corresponding to the mind).

a. Brain (Right and Left)

In the early part of the 20th century, Hans Berger began his work, which eventually led to the creation of the electro-encephalogram.

He is the person who discovered that the brain produces different electrical frequencies: 0 – 4 he called Delta, 4 – 8 Theta, 8 – 12 Alpha and 14 – 28 Beta.

Brain Wave Frequencies

```
28´ ------------------------------------

               BETA


14´ ------------------------------------
12´ ------------------------------------
               ALPHA
 8´ ------------------------------------
               THETA
 4´ ------------------------------------
               DELTA
 0´ ------------------------------------
```

In this theory, the brain is described as a computer that stores information. *All* experience is recorded – every book you've read, every person you've met, every detail of your life – nothing is missing. What is even more amazing is the fact that the brain seems to have no limit to its capacity, at least at the time of this writing, researchers have not discovered any limit.

In its function, the brain is said to be divided: the right side of the brain contains and controls creative, intuitive and subjective activity, while the left side performs logical, rational and objective tasks.

Artists are good examples of people who use right brain activity. They get into a relaxed state, almost like a trance. Their brain frequencies go into the Alpha range and in their mind's eye they can "see" what they want to create. It is the right side of the brain that helps them to perceive and produce objects that have never existed before, objects that are unique and one of a kind.

Women's intuition might be another example of right-brain activity. Women seem to have an innate capacity for picking up information from a distance. For example, a mother may be very involved in the details of a party with a house full of guests. In the midst of all her activity, she senses that her infant is in danger. She drops everything and runs upstairs to the child's room just in time to keep the child from injuring itself. – This kind of knowing is said to be right-brain activity.

Because women in our society are said to be emotional by nature, they are also said to have right brain skills. This, of course, is a generalization and cannot be applied across the board but it is offered here only as an example to help you understand right brain activity.

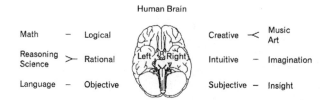

Left brain activity, basically, is found in a traditional educational system of reading, writing and arithmetic. Reading and writing demand that you remember words and phrases so you can understand their meaning. Arithmetic is pure logic.

A lawyer in a court room is a good example of strict use of left brain. What a lawyer does is logically put pieces of a puzzle together following the rules of law. This kind of activity is clearly devoid of emotion and totally involved with logical thought process.

Because men in our society are said to be logical by nature, they are also said to have left brain skills. This, too, is a generalization and cannot be applied to all men, but may help you understand what we mean when using the term "left brain."

b. The Mind (Conscious and Unconscious)

Mind, on the other hand is non-material. It is described as the energy that makes the brain work (as electricity works in a light bulb).

Because scientists do not know the exact nature of matter and its function, they devise theories, which, of course, change in the course of time. In the theory we are now discussing, mind and brain are related in terms of function. For example, the mind is said to be awake when the brain is vibrating at frequencies between 14 and 28 cycles per second. At night, however, when the mind is said to be asleep, the brain frequencies fluctuate from Alpha (between 8' and 12') to Theta (between 4' and 8') and Delta (between 0' and 4') and back again in a pattern that looks like this:

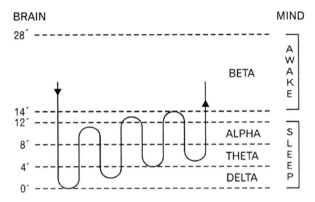

When the brain is functioning at Beta, the mind is limited by time and space. This is the normal waking state we experience every day. It is when we are awake that we have to deal with the material world of food, travel, housing, etc.; constantly watch our clocks for appointments or deadlines, and getting involved in so much that is non-essential.

However, when the brain is functioning at the lower frequencies of Alpha, Theta, and Delta, the mind is not limited by time and space. For example, when you are sitting alone in a park listening to birds, the wind passing through the trees and you relax so that your brain frequencies go below 12 cycles per second, you can enter a state of quiet in which you are free of time and space. In this state, you might find yourself mentally "with" a loved one or in a mental place you might call "euphoria." In this state, you forget about time or space and you seem to be suspended in a "place" of no past, present or future. This kind of experience is so fulfilling that you would like to stay there forever!!! - Usually, experiences like these take place at Alpha (between the brain frequencies of 8 and 12 cycles per second.) "Reverie," "meditation" and "an altered state of consciousness" are terms that point to this kind of experience.

Unconscious activities can be further divided. When the brain is vibrating at Theta frequencies (between 4 and 8 cycles per second) the body is in a very deep state of relaxation in which the person cannot feel physical sensations. This state can be induced by drugs when a patient in hospital is under anesthesia. In this case, the drug slows the brain frequencies to between 4 and 8 cycles so the patient feels no pain. At the same time, the mind is in a "place" similar to that of sleep where there is no time or space.

When the brain vibrates at Delta (between 0 and 4 cycles per second) the person can be in a profound state of sleep or even coma. In this state, the person may be able to receive information from the outside in but cannot communicate from the inside out. Perhaps you have had a similar experience associated with sleep. You begin to wake up but you find that you cannot move any part of your body. Although you are aware and know that you are in bed, you simply cannot move your arm or leg or even your finger. This kind of experience "tells" you that you are in Delta. In this state, you can receive information from the outside but you cannot in any way communicate from the inside out.

If you understand the above experience, you will also realize that it is possible to communicate with persons who are in a coma. Their brain frequencies may be in Delta but they can receive information from the outside. Therefore, touching them and speaking to them in positive and supportive language can help them to recover!

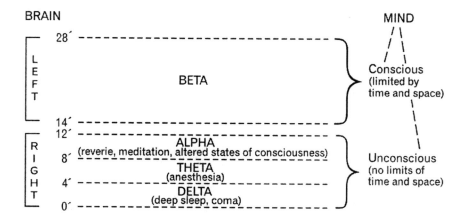

I had the opportunity of working with a young man who had been in a coma for almost two years. After praying with him and explaining how he could speed up his brain frequencies, I told him I was going to count from 1 to 5 and on each number he would speed up his brain frequencies a little more. I explained that at the count of five I would ring a bell and at that moment he would open his eyes and feel fine. When we reached the count of 5 and I rang the bell, he came out of the coma!

In the same way that researchers have found the capacity of the brain to be without limit, they have found the capacity of the mind to be limitless. Although the *conscious* mind is limited by time and space, the *unconscious* mind is not limited.

In sleep, for example, it is possible (and quite common) for individuals to get information about future events. These experiences are referred to as "precognitive dreams." In these kinds of dreams individuals are said to "see into the future" or actually travel to distant places and/or experience distant events.

All of us have these abilities and they are more common than you might imagine. For example, have you ever picked up the phone, knowing who is at the other end? How does this happen? Very simple. The mind is capable of picking up information at a distance and you just "know."

c. The Mind (Super-Conscious)

Penfield, in early experiments, concluded that the *brain* records *every* human experience, nothing is lost. However, most of this information is held in the *unconscious mind*. Only a small portion of this information is accessible to the *conscious mind*. However, it is this huge body of unconscious information that creates the person, functioning at the conscious level.

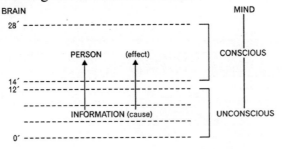

Example: a small child, at the instigation of parents and others, repeats single words and phrases over and over again. Each experience is recorded on the brain and eventually makes a deep impression at the unconscious level. At that point, the child is able to use language effectively and for the most part does not "consciously" recall words and phrases; they simply flow out in the form of speech. Information recorded and stored in the unconscious mind is the *cause*; language at the conscious level is the *effect*.

A logical application of this theory for *you* is this: fill your brain with good, healthy, wholesome, positive thoughts and you will be a good, healthy, wholesome, positive person.

The opposite is also true: fill your mind with evil, sick, base, negative thoughts and you will become an evil, sick, base, negative person.

Although this model explains a good deal of our human experience of habits and automatic skills, it does not explain human creativity.

If the information held in our unconscious minds is gathered from our *personal* experience as an individual, where do we get new ideas that are not part of our personal experience?

In order to answer this question, researchers have coined the term "super-conscious." This term identifies "mind" in possession of all knowledge from the past, present and future, as well as from any place on the planet or in the universe. With the addition of this concept, it is now possible to explain how you and I are able to create new ideas, objects, experiences, etc.

The subdivisions of mind experience can now be identified as (1) conscious, (2) unconscious and (3) super-conscious.

Let us use the example of Michelangelo. He stands in front of a huge piece of marble and decides that he will sculpt the figure of David. This particular image has never existed before, yet somehow Michelangelo can "see" it in his mind's eye.

The explanation is given as follows: Michelangelo is able to tap into the "super-conscious mind" where the image of "David" always exists. This image relays specific information to Michelangelo's brain at either the conscious or the unconscious levels so that his hands will do what is necessary to bring the statue of "David" into reality. We can diagram the process as follows:

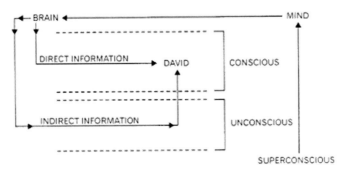

d. Application

The above explanation is very sketchy, to say the least, but we hope it is sufficient for you to understand some of your own personal experience.

i. Conscious Mind

Your body sends a message to your mind that it needs water and you experience "thirst." The mind sends messages to your body and with full awareness, you direct one hand to pick up a glass, direct the other to lift a pitcher and you pour water into a glass. The conscious mind then directs the first hand to bring the glass to your mouth and you drink. (Everything is conscious.)

ii. Conscious and Unconscious Mind

As a typist, you sit down to copy a manuscript. With the conscious mind you concentrate on the *content* of the manuscript, while your unconscious mind directs your fingers to touch the proper keys so that you produce the words that create the manuscript. The *unconscious* mind causes the fingers to function automatically without engaging the conscious mind at all. (One part of the operation is conscious, the other part is unconscious.)

iii. Conscious, Unconscious, and Super-Conscious Mind

Suppose you want to put on a dinner party that is different than anything you have ever experienced. The *conscious* mind begins with ideas from past parties. The *unconscious* mind knows the general pattern of a dinner party and follows that pattern (guests arrive, time for drinks and visiting, followed by eating and finally entertainment). The *super-conscious* mind gets busy giving you new ideas of different combinations of food, unique decorations, new kinds of music and/or entertainment, a completely new guest list, etc. (Conscious, unconscious, and super-conscious mind, together, create something entirely new.)

2. Holographic Theory

The above theory is rather simple and mechanical, but has been used effectively to explain a good deal of human experience. More recently, another theory has been proposed to explain even more of our human experience. This theory is based on the model of a hologram.

a. The Hologram

A hologram is a three-dimensional image of light produced with the use of a laser. A laser beam is directed to a device that can split the beam in two. Part of the beam passes through the device while the other part is reflected in a different direction. The first beam reflects off a set of mirrors so that it eventually falls on the holographic plate. The second beam reflects off an object and then onto the same holographic plate.

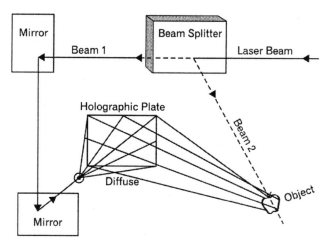

As you can see from the diagram on the previous page, the two sources of light converge before hitting the holographic plate. The interference of both beams mixes the light so that a single image does not appear on the plate (as happens in the case of ordinary photographic film). Instead, the interference pattern creates on the holographic film what looks like a moonscape (irregular circles of all sizes similar to moon craters). When this strange-looking film is placed in front of another laser beam, allowing the light to pass through it, a three-dimensional light-image appears, identical to the original object (an experience much like a "ghost" appearance sometimes portrayed in movies).

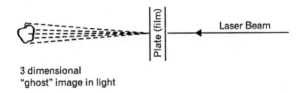

3 dimensional
"ghost" image in light

What is important for our purposes is that somehow the image of the object is contained in every part of the holographic film. For example, if the film is cut up into several pieces, and the laser-light sent through one piece of the film, the complete image of the object continues to appear in three-dimensional form. What this means is that the whole of the object-image is contained in every part of the film.

Another interesting aspect of a hologram is the enormous amount of information that can be stored on a single holographic plate. In the same way that an ordinary photographic film can be exposed several times, so a holographic plate can be exposed several times. However, with ordinary film, several exposures will create a confusing set of images when developed. With a holographic film, however, the results are different. By slightly varying the angle at which the holographic film is exposed and then creating the same angle when the laser is used to project the image, only the image photographed at that angle will appear. Because of this unique characteristic, enormous amounts of information can be recorded and decoded using a single holographic plate. For example, one square inch of holographic film can hold the information equivalent to fifty copies of the bible.

Since the discovery of the hologram in 1947, researchers have applied this model to the brain/mind relationship instead of Theory #1, because it explains more of our human experience.

Now that the hologram has been discovered, researchers have another model to explain the human experience. PLEASE NOTE: the hologram does not completely explain our experience, and as time goes on, this theory too, will be replaced with something more effective.

b. Application

i. The Whole is Contained in Every Part.

This aspect of the hologram can help us better understand how the brain functions. In the past, with the image of the computer to explain the brain, it was thought that certain information was localized in a given part of the brain. But in some cases, individuals, who had brain damage, could recall information that, supposedly, was recorded only on the cells that were destroyed. The holographic model helps us to understand this particular situation. The holographic model helps us to understand by assuming that all the information of the entire brain is in every cell of the brain.

Another assumption previously held by scientists was that a complete brain was necessary for ordinary cognition. However, children who were born hydrocephalic (water on the brain), in some cases, had massive brain damage before excess liquid could be drained from the cerebral cavity. Some of these children recovered with only a small strip of functioning brain matter on either side of the head, or some had only a small section at the top or back of the head. In spite of this massive destruction of brain tissue, these children not only lived to be normal, but went on to become outstanding students at the college and university levels. Again, the holographic model helps us to understand this. If all information and functions of the brain are in every part, then it is logical to understand how a person with brain damage can continue to function normally.

A further application of the holographic model applies to human knowledge. In the past, intelligence was considered to be in the brain only. But scientific evidence now identifies intelligence to be in every part of the body. The holographic model can explain why, for example, when you or I experience a certain odor, memories of past experiences of that odor come to mind. In this case, the information of a past experience seems to be attached to cells in the nose and not only to cells in the brain. The principle being: intelligence is in every part of the body.

Going a step further, the holographic model and the principle of the whole being in every part and every part being in the whole, would seem to indicate that the entire program for the universe is in every human being. This explanation implies that the "creative mind" or the "super-conscious" can be explained in a completely different way. For instance, instead of thinking educationally that a person is born with a blank mind and education impresses information on the mind, we could understand instead that everyone is born with "universal intelligence" and education helps students tap into that unlimited information which is in them from the beginning. For example, why is it that a child, who is exposed from birth to four different languages, will speak four languages? Using the theory given above, we could say that because children are functioning almost entirely at Alpha and Theta frequencies up to age 7 or 8, they are able to tap into "infinite intelligence," be in touch with the "universal program of language" and therefore can master any language.

Please remember, we are trying to understand something that is happening in the world of spirit and it is impossible to adequately express anything in the spirit world. However, the above theory can help us in our understanding, which will never be perfect or complete!

ii. The Seeming Unlimited Capacity of the Brain.

In the hologram, the use of a slightly different angle when impressing new information allows for enormous amounts of material to be recorded in an extremely small space. This image can help us understand how you and I can continue to amass information for a lifetime and still have capacity for more! This image can be an effective aid to better understand how we human beings store information.

iii. Clues to Retrieving Information.

The slightly different angulation when impressing information on a holographic plate allows for the recall of that information when the same angle is used as the laser beam is projected through it.

In our human experience, meditation (or an altered state of consciousness) is one way in which the mind can be "angulated" to perceive whole new levels of information. For example, in the Silva Method of Meditation, one of the exercises directs the students to go to "level" (an altered state of consciousness where brain frequencies are between 8 and 12 cycles per second). In this state, the students are given the name, address, age and sex of a person they have never met and do not know, for example: Johnny Jones, Omaha, NE, age 15, male, This personal information is like the title of a "file." When the student goes into meditation and puts this information on his/her "mental screen", the mind can "find" this file in the storeroom of universal intelligence. The meditator can then "open" this file and immediately get detailed information about the individual: his/her physical description, any physical, psychological, or spiritual problems this subject may have, etc. For example, the meditator can "see" that Johnny Jones has brown hair, a dark complexion, average build, blue eyes, etc. The meditator can also pick up physical problems, like an injured knee or elbow.

In a normal waking state, the average person cannot pick up detailed information like this about another person, but in a meditative state, it happens all the time. Using the theory of the holographic model, we can explain this mental skill by comparing it to the slight angulation of a holographic plate. Meditation causes this "slight angulation" of the mind so that information about the specific person appears on the meditator's mental screen.

The holographic model is a tool to help us to explain how human beings pick up information "at a distance."

Applied to another dimension of our human experience, the holographic model can explain how our physical senses, as well as our minds, can trigger information recall. Some people, for example, get vivid memories of the past, when parts of the body that had been traumatized, are treated by a massage therapist. Experiences like these, tell us that information stored in muscle tissue can be analogous to exposing a holographic plate at a different angle. Physical stimulation of muscle tissue can then become the cause for recalling information stored in this muscle tissue.

Using the holographic model in this way can also explain why you and I learn more easily and more quickly when several senses are activated during the learning process. For example, a child learning the alphabet may have difficulty reciting all 26 letters in their correct order. However, using rhythm and melody, that same child can easily, quickly, and accurately sing the alphabet without any difficulty whatever. The explanation is simple. Sight, sound, speech (and even physical motion), are used to "record" the information into the person of the child. These multiple recordings make it easier to recall because each sense is giving back the same information and the memory is more easily activated. It would be like sending several beams of laser light through a holographic plate and each is exposing the same information.

All this information, and the theories implied, are thoroughly understood by people in advertising. That is why singing commercials are more effective and why television commercials are even more powerful, since they effectively use sight as well as sound with a verbal message.

When I was a child in grade-school, my brother and I had to scrub the kitchen floor each Saturday morning. I made a point of doing my portion of the floor when the radio program "Let's Pretend" was on. The commercial on that program was a little song that I can still remember without difficulty: "Cream of Wheat is so good to eat, yes we have it every day. We sing this song, it will make us strong, and it makes us shout "hurray." It's good for growing babies and grown-ups too to eat. So when you have your breakfast, make sure it's Cream of Wheat." All I have to do is recall the melody and rhythm and the words fall into place easily, quickly and accurately. Even after 60 years, I can still remember all of it (including the experience of scrubbing the kitchen floor!). The holographic model has helped me to understand how this kind of experience happens.

3. Quantum Theory

Physicists have long been examining physical matter. In the past they have studied molecules, then parts of molecules (namely atoms), then parts of atoms (electrons and neutrons) and now are finally getting to the study of the quantum (the smallest particles of matter).

Sometimes experimenters "see" the quantum as a particle. But sometimes they experience it as a wave. In other words, a quantum can be experienced as something physical OR as pure energy. What this means is that the quantum can be a "thing" or it can be "no thing" (pure energy).

The question then is this: Is a quantum some "thing" or is it a purely spiritual reality? Because of this dilemma, physicists now have to be confronted with the dichotomy of matter and spirit in the same way that psychologists have to be confronted with body and mind, and theologians have to be confronted with body and soul.

If you will recall, atoms are made up of tiny particles called electrons that are moving in a circular motion around the nucleus. In this model, the atom is more space than it is matter. But if you go still further into the nucleus to "see" the protons you will experience more of the same; that is, more space than matter. And so it is at every level of physical reality. Scientists tell us that if we could experience reality at the quantum level, we might get the same impression as when we step into a beautifully clear night and look at the sky. What we experience is mostly space with planets and stars taking up a small amount of that space. So too, if we were to "see" our bodies from the quantum level, we would find that 99.99999% of the body is space.

Deepak Chopra explains that the space into which quanta are immersed can be said to be "intelligence." In this way, we can explain how a quantum in the skin knows how to be a skin-quantum, a quantum in the eye knows how to be an eye-quantum, and a quantum in the liver knows how to be a liver-quantum.

Using this image, intelligence (or mind) would have to be perceived as being present throughout the body and not just in the brain (as was described in Theory #1).

At the quantum level, it would be difficult to tell exactly where one body ended and another began, just as it is difficult to tell where one constellation in the sky ends and another begins. "Andromeda," for example, is only a way for humans to designate a section of space in the heavens. The constellation is a reality only in our minds. We have arbitrarily created this group to help us organize the experience of the stars.

Let me use another analogy. The ocean is really only one body of water, but we human beings have put names on different sections of it. We refer, for example, to the Indian Ocean or to the Pacific Ocean, but no one can tell where one begins and the other ends.

If we apply that theory to our bodies, we can say there is intelligence in every cell of the body, but we can also speak of intelligence in each organ of the body, AND when we consider the entire body we say the body has the intelligence of a person. In the same way, we could think of all plants as having "plant intelligence", all animals as having "animal intelligence" and all humans having "human intelligence." If we continue this thought process, it is logical to think also of "universal" intelligence.

Using this model, we have to "see" all of creation surrounded by, or present in, the space we call "intelligence" or "mind." All reality then can be compared to "cosmic soup" or more appropriately "intelligent soup."

For me, the beauty of this theory is that it helps us to perceive the objective reality that there is only one "Mind" or "Intelligence" and that all material things are merely an expression of that Intelligence in a specific time and space. With the help of this model, we can perceive all humanity as a single organism, intimately connected with plant life, animal life and even inanimate matter.

Current sociological phenomenon also seems to indicate that the human race has a common thought process. Marilyn Ferguson, for example, in her book "Aquarian Conspiracy," reports how small groups of people all over the planet are "seeing" the need to create love and understanding as a means toward world peace, instead of war and competition. These groups are in no way organized, nor are they part of a single network. They simply spring up because of a common thought process. Since the work of Marilyn Ferguson, all kinds of "support groups" and/or "small faith communities" have sprung up all over the world: meditation support groups, charismatic communities, etc.

Using concepts from Quantum Theory we can explain this phenomenon by saying that because Intelligence is "one", an idea generated by one person can be picked up by another (since all are part of the "one Intelligence").

Let me use an analogy. Consider your body to be a universe in itself, made up of innumerable quanta immersed in intelligence. You are walking down the street and immediately behind you a firecracker goes off. Your entire body reacts instantaneously; you physically jump, your heart begins to pump, blood pressure goes up, hands sweat, etc. It is as if "Intelligence" throughout the body has picked up the message and, at the same instant, all parts of your body react together. (It is not as if there is communication from the ears to the brain and then from the brain to the rest of the body. There simply is no lapse of time to allow for the reaction.) "One Intelligence" communicates simultaneously with each individual quantum and there is a single reaction.

Some years ago I remember looking up at the sky seeing a flash of some kind. As I watched, I realized that I was seeing a flock of birds. At one moment they all shifted their flight pattern exactly the same way at exactly the same time and the light of the sun reflected on their shiny feathers to create the "flash." Then, just as suddenly, they shifted their pattern of flight and the entire flock seemed to disappear. I wondered how hundreds of birds could know to move in exactly the same way at the same time. This theory of "Universal Intelligence" and Quantum Theory is one way of helping us to understand these experiences.

a. Wave or Particle

When scientists analyze reality, they speak in terms of smaller and smaller parts, e.g. cells, molecules, atoms, electrons, and finally, quanta. At this basic quantum level there is a unique phenomenon that takes place. Sometimes the quantum functions like a wave; sometimes it functions like a particle.

At present, scientists do not know how this happens, but they do know it is real. But how can a wave (pure energy) all of a sudden become a particle? That would be tantamount to saying that some *thing* comes from *no thing*.

In the ordinary order of things, we can explain how one thing can come from another, for example, how trees produce seeds and generate other trees or how wood can be transformed into a piece of furniture. But if we move in the opposite direction, we have to get to the first tree or the first seed. But where does this "first" come from?

Quantum physics explains the situation in this way. When the human mind (which is one with "Universal Mind") expects to "see" a quantum as a particle, that thought process changes pure energy into a particle. But when the human mind expects to "see" a wave, the quantum "shows up" as a wave. What Quantum Physics is saying is this: using the power of mind, human beings are co-creators with "Universal Intelligence" in being able to bring some "thing" into reality from the "sea of consciousness" rather than bringing something from some other "thing." Deepak Chopra in his book "Quantum Healing" describes the process this way: "The whole picture is like a bucket brigade, where each fireman gets his bucket from the fireman before him, except for the first, who get his from nowhere." - It seems to me that what we may be dealing with here is the very act of creation.

I think that Pierre Teilhard de Chardin may have been referring to this kind of reality when he explained from a philosophical point of view: all that is needed for something to happen, or for a situation to change, or for a material object to appear is that one person have a thought to that effect, and with the passage of a sufficient amount of time, the reality will materialize.

Is this what Jesus was talking about when he pointed to "oneness" saying: "I and the Father are One", and "I am the vine, you are the branches", and "That they all may be one as we Father are one"? – Is this what Buddha experienced in meditation when he explained how meditation can connect us all with "no thing" which in fact is "Universal Intelligence"? – Is this what the Saints and Holy People of all religions experienced when they went into ecstasy?

Our minds are a great gift. It is this faculty by which we become one with Universal Intelligence and all of reality. It is by means of this faculty that we become co-creators with Universal Intelligence to shape our lives, our world and the universe. But our minds are also a great mystery, one that we will never be able to fully comprehend!!!

b. Application

i. Global Village

Quantum Theory can be applied in very practical ways to explain important global events. For 50 years, Russia ruled over Eastern Europe. During those years millions of people prayed for and visualized peace. Then, all of a sudden on Nov. 9, 1989 the Berlin Wall came down. This is only one example of how collective thought process creates reality.

If you understand this example, then you will understand the principle that "thoughts we generate today create the reality we experience tomorrow."

This is the concept of the hundredth monkey. As the story goes, monkeys on an isolated island were in the habit of eating their food wherever they found it. Then one day, one of the monkeys discovered that by washing the sand off the food it tasted better and was easier to eat. Other monkeys, seeing this monkey washing food, began to wash their food too. When the majority of the monkeys on the island began to wash their food, all of a sudden on another island, completely isolated from the first, the monkeys there began to wash their food. – The moral of the story is that when a sufficient number of people think in a given way, it will have an effect on the entire population. Quantum Theory can help us to understand this process and use it in a positive direction.

The same theory explains the power of prayer. The scientific community has created experiments to prove the power of prayer. Heart patients, all having the same difficulties and procedures, were divided into two groups. One group had people praying for them but neither the patient nor the people praying knew each other; nor did they know about the experiment. The other group was not prayed for. This experiment was done several times and, in each case, the patients who were prayed for healed faster than those who were not prayed for. The Quantum Theory can also be used to explain this kind of situation.

I believe we are at a point in our evolution when we must come to understand that the thought process going on in one part of the planet necessarily has an effect on the thought process of all humanity. We are not isolated individuals on this planet; we are part of an amazing "Whole." We must pick up the responsibility of sharing and shaping a global thought process that will be *beneficial for every living creature* on the planet.

When we come to know the power of thought, and how we are linked together in the reality of "Universal Intelligence," it will be important to explain the process to peoples all over the world, especially our youth. Imagine what kind of progress we could make in the peace process, by creating structures in education to facilitate ongoing instruction in this area of human development, and to create suitable teaching strategies to activate mind energy on a global level! I do believe that "what we can conceive in our minds, and believe, is possible!"

ii. Universal Awareness

If the thought process of our planet is one with the thought process of the universe, we will also have to extend our awareness to issues that are not merely global but, indeed universal. Perhaps this is one of the new frontiers that will have to be explored by the upcoming generation and an area of responsibility that will have to be picked up by world government.

It is interesting to note that individuals who have been in outer space and who see Planet Earth from that perspective have a dramatic shift in awareness. Capt. Edgar Mitchell, for example, was so changed by his experience as an astronaut that he began the Institute of Noetic Science to help bridge the gap between science and religion. His passion for expansive awareness and truth is helping individuals all over the planet to "see" the unity he saw.

When leaders of nations have this kind of perception, they will be asking "is this good for the world?" instead of asking "is this good for our country?" When religious leaders develop this kind of awareness, they will be asking: "How can we share our truth with the world?" instead of: "does this truth fit into our system of theology." When people in the business world create a world view they, too, will ask; "how can we share our wealth with the people who buy our products?" instead of asking "how can we make more money?"

iii Health Implications

Our thoughts are a prominent factor in the functioning of the immune system. The science of psycho-neuro-immunology has proven this fact in controlled experiments. What this means for you and me is this: controlling our thoughts and giving them a push in a positive direction is an essential element in preventive healthcare, as well as healing. In his book, "Biology of Belief," Bruce Lipton, Ph.D., says:

"You can live a life of fear or live a life of love. You have the choice! But I can tell you that if you choose to see a world full of love, your body will respond by growing in health. If you choose to believe that you live in a dark world full of fear, your body's health will be compromised as you physiologically close yourself down in a protection response."

Some years ago a medical doctor, who had high blood pressure problems, came into my Silva Meditation Class. I spoke about using mental pictures of quiet scenes like lying on a beach on a beautiful summer day, or sitting in a fishing boat on a calm lake, or walking through a beautiful woods, and how these thoughts can cause physical and mental relaxation. He began to use relaxation exercises on a daily basis and was able to bring his blood pressure back to normal without any medication whatsoever. Since that time, he has sent some of his patients to our Center to get a recorded relaxation exercise so they, too, can learn how to lower blood pressure without the use of drugs.

Bernie Siegel in his book "Love, Medicine and Miracles," documents many cases of patients who were able to overcome ill health and disease by simply shifting their thought process.

The human mind is perhaps our most powerful ally on our journey through life but especially in our efforts to be healthy. Unfortunately, our educational system does not teach students about this unlimited reservoir, much less show them how to use it. Because of this deficiency in our systems, I have dedicated the last 30 years of my life to traveling all over the world to educate people of all ages about this important aspect of our human dimension and to show them how to use this power to set goals for their lives, how to use mind to solve problems, and how to stay in touch mentally with all that is good, true and beautiful.

4. Conclusion

New theories continue to appear, for example, String Theory, but remember always, no theory will be able to give us a complete understanding of the world in which we live. In the end we find it is all a mystery that boggles the mind, stimulates our interest and motivates professionals to continue to study and explore.

This kind of study continues in the fields of education, economics, medicine, religion and every other aspect of human experience. Think of it, we will have something to study as long as there are human beings on the planet!!!

Before we close this chapter, let me state once again the fact that there is a built-in difficulty in studying anything about our world, especially the non-material world. Our world is without limit, therefore, any statement, however informed, will always be inadequate. That means all that I have said is woefully inadequate! The only thing I can do here is present some basic ideas from present theories with the hope that you, the reader, will have some foundation for understanding the following chapters and their application.

Take from what I have written anything that may be useful for you. If something does not "work" for you intellectually, psychologically or spiritually, let it go and seek to clarify your reality as best you can. Your job is to create some understanding that will give meaning and direction to your life – a task that only you can perform for yourself!

The theories given here are only aids to understanding the vast amount of knowledge that is coming from research and personal experience. You can count on these theories to be updated soon and continue to be updated for the rest of your life.

Think in terms of transportation: human beings have come from walking, to riding on the backs of animals, to using carts, then bicycles, then motorized vehicles, then balloons and eventually aircraft and now space craft. Who knows, maybe before too long we will be "beamed" from place to place!!!

In the same way as changes continue to take place in travel, so will changes take place in the understanding and the use of "Mind."

Human beings do not have all the answers and never will!!! However, it is our nature to move into the future seeking more and more understanding. As we do this, we change and adjust our theories realizing full well that no theory is perfect.

Given the above, we need not despair about limited understanding of things spiritual. Remember, although intellectual knowing is limited, experiential knowing is not. Experience is another valid way of knowing, but it is always direct and complete. For example, you could study the 5th Symphony of Beethoven for your entire lifetime and not understand all of the relationships that exist there between individual notes, different scales, different dynamics, melodies, rhythms, etc. However, when you experience this composition, you get a feeling, an emotional experience that is direct and complete. You will never be able to express in words what this experience is but you "know" it is something important, something powerful and something that can dramatically change your life.

Through the centuries, the masters of the spiritual life have tried to help us. For example, Jesus used comparison when he referred to the spirit world as "The Kingdom of God" and "The Kingdom of Heaven." In Matthew 13:31 he said: "The kingdom of heaven is like a grain of mustard seed, which a man took and sowed in his field. It is the smallest of all seeds; but when it is grown, it is larger than all of the herbs; and it becomes a tree, so that the birds of the air come and nest in its branches."

The Buddha and Jesus not only spoke about going into the quiet where we would experience the "Kingdom," they both gave us examples of how to sit in quiet, how to go to a garden or a mountain top and there, entirely alone, experience "Divine Presence." In the Franciscan Order, when we were in novitiate training, we had to rise at 11:45 pm and go to the chapel to chant the Divine Office for one hour. Of course in those days, everything was chanted in Latin (most of which I did not understand). I can speak from first-hand experience: after chanting in Latin for one hour, we were definitely in an altered state of consciousness. We were so relaxed we got very close to sleep and sometimes fell asleep (standing up!!!). Immediately after the hour of chanting, we had one-half hour for formal meditation. Often during that time, I could not tell you if my feet were on the floor, or if they were even there! Often that half hour seemed like 2 minutes. Sometimes, I felt as if I were floating in a sea of Love. These kinds of experience in the spirit world changed my life forever. In that state, I could clearly "see" what my future was to be, I could find solutions to problems in my life, and I could anchor my earthly life in experiences of love and peace.

In the Sufi tradition we are told that we can get this experience by dancing. When I was a child, growing up in a Polish community in Omaha, Nebraska, weddings and other celebrations were never without music and dancing. Some of the older women had difficulty getting around and often used a cane. But, at a wedding or a shower, these same women put their canes in a corner and moved to the dance floor. There they seemed to enter another dimension of reality. With poker-like faces they "floated" around the floor, almost in a state of rapture. As a small child, having the opportunity to dance with these women, I, too, began to fall into that same state and learned first hand how euphoric one can get when caught up in the experience of music and dance!

The remainder of this book is dedicated to helping you not merely to understand meditation and its allied experiences, but more importantly, to lead you into the practice of various techniques for deep human knowing and understanding.

5. Suggested Activities for Chapter II

1. To get in touch with spiritual reality daily, try using this morning
   schedule:
   > When you awaken, remain in bed for 5 or 10 minutes.
   > Lie flat on your back with your hands at your side.
   > Close your eyes.
   > Mentally count downward from 30 to 1 several times
   > (mentally picture the numbers as neon signs atop a

building in the middle of the night or see them on steps as you mentally descend a staircase or mentally hear the numbers spoken aloud by yourself or someone else).

After repeating the countdown several times, lie quietly and pay attention to how you feel.

Open your eyes and get out of bed.

2. Find a comfortable position in a quiet place and close your eyes.

    a. Recall a past experience that was peaceful or happy (recall as much detail as you can).

    b. With your eyes still closed, pay attention to the fact that the "I" of the past is the same as the "I" of the present.

    c. Pay attention to how you feel.

    d. Open your eyes.

3. Find a comfortable position in a quiet place. Turn on some relaxing music and spend 10 or 15 minutes listening.

Pay attention to the fact that you and the music are one in the experience.

At the end of the exercise, open your eyes and pay attention to how you feel.

4. If you are not familiar with courses in meditation, get a copy of book "The Silva Method" and/or find out if a class is being given in your area. Look up the website www.thesilvamethod.com

III

MEDITATION

When I first joined the Franciscan Order, I immediately became aware that meditation was something important – an essential part of the daily schedule. Every morning before breakfast the community gathered in the chapel to chant Morning Prayer, and after that we had a half-hour of meditation. This routine of morning and evening meditation was required (by law) of every priest, nun and religious brother the world over.

1. Understanding Meditation

What is meditation? How do you describe or understand it? In the "Encyclopedic Dictionary of Religion" it states:

Meditation is a "form of reflective mental prayer, usually called discursive in distinguishing it from other forms of prayer ... it proceeds from an analysis of truths, or comparison of realities, to their application to the one meditating."

"The New Catholic Encyclopedia" defines meditation as:

"A form of mental prayer consisting in devout reflection aimed at arousing the will to acts of fervor."

I don't know how you react to these definitions, but I am immediately confused. What does "analysis of truth" mean? Or what is "comparison of realities?" (What realities?) I didn't know what "acts of fervor" were much less how to "arouse" them! Nor did I have a clue as to what a "devout reflection" was.

These definitions were confusing for me, at best! They certainly did not give me any help in doing meditation. I got the idea it was supposed to be a mental exercise of some kind, a time to think about the lives of the saints or "holy things." Perhaps it was supposed to be just another theology class, but this time on our knees!

I followed the directions, of course, thinking that perhaps by practice I would come to understand. I realize now that a great deal of the problem was the theological language. I just didn't know what the words meant. Even when I asked questions of our professors, I could not get clear answers. It seemed to me they were simply restating what they had learned from their teachers without fully understanding it themselves.

It was not until I was a priest for more than 12 years, and a friar for more than 20 years that I came in touch with the Silva Method of Meditation. Mario DiCicco, a fellow friar and a close friend of many years, was stationed in Chicago. He had seen an ad in the newspaper announcing a free lecture, as well as a four-day class that was to follow. He phoned me in Cleveland where I was living and asked if I would be interested in joining him for the first weekend of this class. Luckily I did not have commitments for those few days so I got permission from my Guardian and went to Chicago.

It was this weekend that opened my eyes to the exact meaning of meditation and was the weekend that was to change the entire course of my life.

The course used precise terms to describe the experience of meditation. "Close your eyes, take a deep breath, and while exhaling mentally repeat and visualize the number 3 three times..."

The instructor used detailed charts and scientific terms to explain physical and mental relaxation. "When you are in your normal waking state," he explained, "your brain frequencies are above 14 cycles per second, but as you relax and enter the meditative state, your brain frequencies slow down below 14 cycles. In scientific terms, this state is called 'Alpha'."

Besides the precise language, the course is a wonderful blend of theory and practice. For example, the course begins with a description of *physical* relaxation - how to relax the body by simply concentrating on each individual part, from head to toes. After the explanation, we were taken through a relaxation exercise: Close your eyes, take a deep breath and concentrate on relaxing your scalp ... relax your forehead ... relax your eyelids ... etc.

Then came a description of *mental* relaxation and how it can be achieved by imagining yourself in a place where you are completely relaxed. The exercise followed: "Close your eyes and picture yourself at the beach on a warm summer day ... imagine sounds of the surf ... imagine the blue sky and a few fluffy clouds ... feel the sun on your skin ..."

It was this combination of clear explanation of theory and the immediate application in practice that gave me the understanding, which my theological professors simply did not have.

How then can meditation be defined? *Theologically*, meditation can be described as a state of physical and mental relaxation in which a person can become aware of, and experience the Divine Presence within. *Scientifically*, meditation can be described as a state of physical and mental relaxation in which a person can experience Mind at the unconscious level (where all limits of time and space disappear) and where a person can experience all that is True, Good and Beautiful.

For me, the scientific terminology makes the reality much clearer. In traditional theological language, for example, meditation is described as an "inward attitude" or "attentive spontaneity." For anyone in this day and age, these terms can be very ambiguous. I think science is making a great contribution to the field of Mystical Theology by describing these human experiences in clear and concise language for those of us living in a scientific age.

a. A State of Being

Please note that the descriptions above speak of a *"state"* in which a person can experience God or a *"state"* in which a person can experience all that is True, Good and Beautiful."

Among the different "states" in which humans can exist, the scientific community distinguishes between "a normal waking state" and "an altered state."

Let me use two examples. Imagine yourself in downtown New York. You have to concentrate on a great deal: the people around you, the pavement you are walking on, the traffic at intersections, traffic lights, etc. In this "state" you can experience stress as you pay attention to what you must do each moment, concentration on your destination, etc. In this state, brain frequencies are somewhere between 14 and 28 cycles per second and your awareness is limited and focused on a particular time and space. This is referred to as the "normal waking state."

Now imagine yourself out in the country, far from the city where the only sounds are birds, the rustling of leaves in the trees, a breeze rushing through pine trees, a babbling brook, etc. You are seated under a tree completely relaxed, aware of the beauty of the landscape and feeling no stress at all. Your mind wanders to friends miles away, or to pleasant times when you were a child, or to family and friends who have died but who even now enrich your life. In this state, brain frequencies are below 14 cycles per second and the thought process is free of all limits of time and space. This is referred to as "an altered state." Meditation belongs to this second category. It is considered to be an altered state of being (or awareness).

b. Physical and Mental Relaxation

Physical relaxation is a basic prerequisite for entering a meditative state. It may seem a simple matter, but in our present society, physical relaxation can be a real challenge for many people. Because lifestyles today are so active and intense, stress is common, even among children. For this reason, whenever I am teaching meditation, I spend a great deal of time on relaxation. In The Silva Method, for example, a four-hour block of time is dedicated to explaining and experiencing deep relaxation.

There are a number of methodologies for relaxation and one approach can be as effective as the next. You can, for example, find a comfortable position, close your eyes, take a deep breath and then concentrate on different parts of your body, relaxing each as you go. You may begin at the top of your head and move downward until you get to the tips of your toes.

I prefer to use this downward movement because it is consistent with other processes in the body. For example, as you relax, the temperature of the body slows, the breathing mechanism slows down, the heart rate decreases, the metabolism slows down, brain frequencies go down, etc.

It is possible, however, for the exercise to begin at the toes and move upward to the top of the head.

Another technique is to count down from 30 to 1 or from 60 to 1 and mentally tell yourself that on each descending number you are more and more relaxed.

Still another technique suggests that you tighten individual muscles and then feel them relax. Tighten and relax until every muscle is completely relaxed and at rest.

Mental relaxation is achieved by filling the mind with images of a place or situation that reflects peace and tranquility. For example, imagine yourself on a leisurely walk through a beautiful garden. You can see a bright blue sky, hear the sound of birds, feel the warm sun, and smell the gentle scent of blossoms...you imagine yourself completely at rest and at peace.

This may sound like a simple procedure, but in the context of present-day society, it may not be that easy. So many people today are constantly preoccupied with problems, responsibilities, commitments and challenges. For some, it may take a great deal of effort to focus on a scene like the one I just described.

In his book "Psycho-Cybernetics," one of the early classics by Maxwell Maltz, the author suggests that you create a special place in your imagination, a room with a beautiful view. Every time you want to go into meditation, he suggests that you recall this room in all its detail.

Jose Silva suggests that you create your own "ideal place of relaxation" for the same purpose.

Remember, both physical and mental relaxation are necessary for effective meditation.

c. One Experience, Many Descriptions

The experience of being in an altered state of consciousness is natural to all human beings. In fact, it is necessary for relieving stress and valuable for promoting health.

A woman, for example, who works professionally, cares for a child, picks up responsibilities of married life, works in the community, etc., is constantly "on the go." This lifestyle can create a great deal of stress. When stress builds, a person will have a need to find a quiet place and relax. The woman in question may be driving by a park on the way home and have the urge to stop. She parks the car, sits on a bench or a swing, and just "hangs out" for 10 or 15 minutes. After a short time of quiet, she feels revitalized and is ready to get back to her busy life, now feeling relaxed and refreshed.

Or a man, overwhelmed with the responsibilities of work, the stress of marriage and family, commitments with children and church, feels a need to take a few hours off on Saturday. He gets into a boat at a nearby pond with a fishing pole and in the quiet is calmed and re-energized.

Even children will get off by themselves, perhaps in a large box or in a closet, to find quiet where they can relax and simply "be."

Whether you refer to the experience of quiet as being "meditation" and/or "an altered state of consciousness" does not really matter. The experience is the same. What saints and theologians call "mystical experiences" are identical to what the scientists call "psychic experience." Words do not change the human experience.

Of course, the saints and holy people of all major religions who developed these skills had many and varied experiences. St. Clare, for example, who lived in the early 1200s and who was an intimate friend of St. Francis, was skilled in the discipline of meditation. One Christmas Eve she was ill and could not attend the midnight Mass at the Basilica of St. Francis on the other side of the city. The rest of the sisters attended the service and when they returned they wanted to give Clare all the details of the celebration. However, while the Liturgy was in process, Clare had gone into meditation and was able to "see" and "hear" everything, although she was not physically there. This phenomenon is referred to as a "vision" or "remote viewing." Because of this kind of experience, St. Clare was chosen to be the patron of "tell-a-vision."

The experience of St. Clare is essentially the same as a psychic who is able to go into an altered state of consciousness and help police find a missing child or a criminal. In scientific language, however, we refer to this skill as "remote viewing" but it is essentially the same as the "vision" experience of Clare and happens in the same way.

It seems to me that, at this time in history, the worlds of science and theology are coming together in a way that has not happened before. It is a wonderful time because science is giving us a universal language to describe these phenomena and the field of theology is giving the documentation and the experience of the saints, which can be studied by science.

My point in all this is, the human experience is the same whether you describe it in theological terms or whether you describe it in scientific terms.

d. Heightened Awareness

During meditation, the body is in a state of physical relaxation and functions differently than it does in a normal waking state. The breathing slows down, the heart rate slows down, metabolism slows down, body temperature lowers, brain waves decrease, etc.

So, too, during meditation the mind functions differently. In a normal waking state the mind is limited by time and space, as well as, many other limits. However, in meditation, the mind can be free of all limits, including those of time and space.

This means that in meditation the mind can move forward and backward in time or from any point on the planet to any other point in the universe. For example, it is not uncommon for people in this heightened state of awareness to know who is on the other end of the phone before they pick up the receiver. Nor is it uncommon for a mother in one part of the house to know immediately that her infant at the other end of the house is in danger. Sometimes these experiences are put into the category of "intuition."

The Saints and Holy People of all religions became skilled in the art of meditation and exhibited what can be called "mystic" or "psychic" phenomena. The Cure of Ars, for example, was able to read the minds and hearts of people who came to him for counseling or advice. St. Joan of Arc was able to hear voices of those who had died. St. John, the Apostle, had visions that are clearly described in the Book of Revelations.

Many others have had these same experiences because they were skilled at entering an altered state to consciousness. Nostradamus, for example, was able to predict far into the future. Einstein obtained the Theory of Relatively in this state. Thomas Edison called his experience "consulting his board of directors."

Some of these kinds of experiences can happen in sleep also. Because brain frequencies are below 14 cycles during sleep, exactly the same way as they are in meditation, it is possible for any of us to have "heightened awareness" in dreams. For example, my aunt had a recurring dream of a chariot coming from the sky and picking up someone from the family and then returning back into the sky. Whenever she had this dream, someone from the family died the next day. One morning she awoke, remembering this same dream. At breakfast she told her husband and her only son about the dream and asked them to be careful. Later that morning her son was accidentally shot in the back of the head by a friend who was playing with a new gun.

These kinds of experiences are not new or unique. In the Old Testament, for example, Daniel interpreted the dreams of King Nebuchadnezzar. In the New Testament Joseph was told in a dream to flee into Egypt so that the life of Jesus could be saved. Experiences like these are still common today, but not too many people talk about them.

As a five-year-old child in the first grade, I remember listening to a Friar Priest who came into the class to talk about St. Francis and about Franciscans. When he finished, he asked the class, "Who of you boys would like to be a Franciscan Priest?" I put up my hand and at that moment knew for certain that in my adult life I would be a Franciscan Priest. It was years later that I learned from my study of meditation that children up to about 7 or 8 years of age are almost always in a meditative state (with brain frequencies below 14 cycles). Only then did I understand how I could have known at that early age what my future life was to be.

Please note that these phenomena are not the most important part of meditation and/or dreams; nor are they essential to meditation. However, they are valuable and useful in helping us to deal with life, especially when it gets difficult or challenging!

What I believe is most important for people like you and me is that meditation is the place where we can "be" in our most perfect human state. When we are relaxed and quiet, we can "see" life as it really is and be able to deal with it more efficiently and effectively. For example, when someone called my aunt at work to notify her of her son's death, before any information was given to her, she said: "It's Richard, isn't it?" That dream had prepared her for a very difficult life experience and she was prepared to deal with it.

Meditation can be used in unlimited ways and in common everyday life situations. A student who knows how to use meditation before and after study, as well as during exams, will learn faster and recall information easier. Just the other day, I got a letter from a 12-year-old who had been in one of my classes a few months ago. He told me how he was able to go into meditation when he could not remember the answer to a particular question while taking an exam. Every time he relaxed, went into a meditative state and asked for the answer, it popped into his head. Using meditation in this way, he was able to improve his grades significantly. The fact is, when we are relaxed and calm, our minds function more efficiently and effectively.

I believe that many people in our society cannot make appropriate decisions about their future lives because they do not take the time to quiet themselves first. If they did, they could experience a "heightened awareness" that could bring clear direction into their lives, as well as solutions to daily problems and challenges.

2. Meditation as Experience

When I first came in touch with meditation in the Friary, it consisted of three separate activities: 1) a reading, 2) the meditation itself, and 3) an application.

Usually we gathered in the chapel and began by chanting the Psalms for at least 15 or 20 minutes. This activity would get us relaxed. After that a reading was done by one of the friars, which lasted about ten minutes. Typically this reading was a short section from the life of a saint whose feast we were celebrating that day, or a discussion of a specific virtue like patience or kindness.

When the reading was completed, we knelt (or sat) in quiet for about 20 minutes. During this time we were told to "consider" the material and/or to "look for its meaning." As I said previously, I thought it was supposed to be a mental exercise of some kind.

Before the meditation time was over, we were to come up with some kind of practical application. For example, if the meditation was about the loving attitude of a particular saint, we were to think how we could follow the example of the saint and put more acts of love into our own lives. Or if the meditation was on patience, we were to plan how we ourselves could be more patient. The goal, of course, was to improve ourselves and the quality of our lives.

This three-step approach was a plan created by St. Peter of Alcantara (1499-1562) and followed by Franciscans all over the world for centuries.

The daily experience of being in sustained quiet was relaxing and pleasant, sometimes deeply satisfying, and occasionally profoundly moving. I remember one day in the novitiate (a year of strict training) when I was getting fed up with the daily routine, the plain food, shaving with cold water, bathing only once a week, etc. etc. I went into evening prayer feeling frustrated and depressed, and wondering how much more I could take. As we started the chanting, I began to relax and a great calm came over me. That evening the meditation was on the presence of God, and in the quiet that followed, I began to *feel* the presence of God. A peace settled over me and I wanted to stay in that quiet forever! When the meditation period was over, I went to supper with a heart filled with joy and the knowledge that the difficulties of my life didn't mean much at all, compared to what I had just experienced. I was able, once again, to see my ideals as well as the clear purpose of my life.

It is because of "happenings" like this, that we all went back to meditation again and again. Those exceptional experiences did not occur daily, not even often, but when they did we all knew something personally about the world of Spirit – something wonderful and powerful!!

When, however, I learned the Silva techniques for getting into meditation, I began to experience that state of euphoria much more frequently and now, after much practice, almost daily.

3. Active and Passive Meditation

We have mentioned that meditation is a state of physical and mental relaxation in which we become aware of God's presence or where we experience Mind at the unconscious level. The question now arises, "What do you do in meditation? How does it affect our daily lives?" As I see it, there are basically two kinds of meditation, active and passive.

a. Active Meditation

Active meditation can be described as taking control of the thought process and giving it direction. For example, suppose Gertrude wants to be more patient with her five-year old son, Johnny. She goes into meditation and pictures herself in familiar situations in which she has been impatient with Johnny. Then she begins to use her creative imagination and mentally sees herself speaking to her son in a low-pitched and soft voice. She visualizes herself interacting with Johnny in a kind and patient manner. These images get impressed on Gertrude's brain and when repeated often enough, become part of her unconscious. When that happens, she wakes up one day and finds herself being patient with her son without even thinking about it. She begins to act the way she pictured herself in meditation (see the diagram on page 20 of Chapter II).

This example, Gertrude gives direction to her thoughts. She is the active agent for producing a specific result. In this kind of meditation there is a clearly defined goal and the meditator is the instrument for directing the inner Energy of God, or Mind, to make the goal become a reality.

Please note, this kind of meditation can be used only when the end result is clear. It is then that active meditation (at an Alpha state) can have a direct effect on life (at the Beta state) and the person meditating becomes what he/she thinks about.

I want to make it clear that, although we describe meditation as being the result of Gertrude's thought process and intention, she is always working with the Spirit dimension of her person (which can also be defined as God). It is impossible for Gertrude to be separated from that in her, which is Spirit. She, therefore, is working always *with* God to create the end result.

If you recall, Jesus said: "The Kingdom of God is here at hand. It is within." He also taught that "I and the Father are one," and "I am the vine, you are the branches." He was constantly trying to clarify that He and God are one and that *we* and God are one. St. Paul, understanding this process said: "I can do all things in Christ who strengthens me."

Active meditation is a very efficient model in which you and God can do anything! Essentially, the Silva Method and that of St. Peter of Alcantara are examples of this meditation technique.

b. Passive Meditation

Passive meditation, on the other hand, has a completely different purpose. Sometimes in life, we simply do not know what the end result is supposed to be, or we do not have the solution to a problem or challenge in our lives. In these cases, passive meditation can be more effective.

Let me use another example. Suppose Joe is unhappy with his job and knows that he must move into another position, but doesn't know exactly where he should go or what he should do. It is at a time like this that Joe can effectively use passive meditation.

This kind of meditation can be described as going into the Alpha state simply to "be." In this state, Joe does not give direction to his thought process. In fact, he does just the opposite. He lets go of the thought process and allows it to happen. This is mental prayer in which he "lets go and lets God."

While sitting in the quiet, Joe can center himself in Divine Presence (Spirit or Mind) and wait. In this place of quiet, thoughts come and eventually a clear goal appears and/or a solution to a problem unfolds. In this case, Joe is a passive agent and God (Spirit or Mind) is the active agent. Because the communication takes place in Joe's mind, this kind of meditation is also known as "mental" prayer.

Let me share another example. When I was teaching compulsory General Music at the high-school level in an all-boys facility, I was trying to figure out how to get my students involved and interested at the very beginning of the year. One day in meditation, as I sat paying attention only to my breath, thoughts began to flood my mind. I saw myself playing a recording of music selections that I would be using during the year. I could "see" students marching to a brass band, balloons, bubbles, laughter, dancing, etc. To be honest, it frightened me and I was thinking: "If I tried something like this the staff would consider me to be crazy!" However, when I shared some of these ideas with my associate, Carole, she got all excited and began to add her own creativity to the "show." -- We did create this "happening" which became so effective that we were asked to write it up for a music journal. In the end, we got letters from all over the country and were thrilled to have helped other teachers get their students excited about a General Music Class. - All of the above was possible, only because of an experience I received in meditation!!!

Passive meditation can also be used to bring the meditator into direct contact with "Peace," "Beauty," "Truth" or "Ultimate Reality." Transcendental Meditation, Zen, certain kinds of Yoga, and in the Christian tradition, the "Prayer of Quiet" are all means of getting into a state of passive meditation. Experiences in this state can be profound and life transforming.

My Uncle Joe was a fun loving person and a wonderful party host. For many years, he owned a little cabin outside of Omaha, Nebraska. There was a pond on the property for swimming, boating and fishing and the extended family had an open invitation every weekend during the summer months. Uncle Joe was an expert at barbequing ribs, which he cooked while he drank beer and sang songs, some in Polish, some in German and others in Italian, English and even Swedish. But Uncle Joe was a hard worker too. He worked for 30 years at the Court House well into his 70s. When Uncle Joe grew older, in his 90s, he was in a nursing home. The nurses put him into a chair each morning and he always requested that he be able to look out the window at the lawn, trees, etc. One day I went to visit him and found to my amazement that he wasn't interested in watching TV or in reading books or magazines. He was completely satisfied just looking out the window. He told me that when he got quiet, his mind took him to a place where he was "full up!" He didn't want or need anything else. This is the state I am talking about. A state in which a person is so "full", he/she doesn't want or need anything else. It really is a taste of "heaven."

Active and passive meditation are ancient forms of "mental prayer" and are described in the Western tradition of mysticism by many saints. Theresa of Avila, for example, used the image of a castle in her meditations. In this castle she had individual rooms where she could work on specific aspects of her life. For example, if she wanted to be patient, she would picture herself in the "patient" room, practicing how to develop this particular virtue. If she wanted to be happy, she would mentally go into the "happy" room. These are examples of how she used active meditation.

In the center of her castle, she had a room where she would go simply to "be" with God. It was in this mental "space", where she was able to do what I am calling "passive meditation," where she could receive direction and guidance, and where she could simply "be" with all that is True, Good and Beautiful.

The following outline may help you to understand how these different forms fit under the general heading of Prayer.

PRAYER OUTLINE

Please note that vocal prayer, meditation and contemplation all fit under the category of <u>PRAYER</u>. All are important and valuable, but each fills a different need and has a different purpose.

Vocal prayer is the simplest. The language of vocal prayer is "words." Traditionally, it has been described as "talking to God" in the same way you would talk to another human being. This approach can be taught easily to children or beginners in the spiritual life.

As individuals mature spiritually, they naturally move toward Mental Prayer (usually to Meditation first and then to Contemplation). You will note that the language of Active Mental Prayer (Meditation) is "images." In Passive Mental Prayer (Contemplation) there is no language. It is simply "being" with God (Spirit).

Vocal prayer can be used effectively to bring a group of people together mentally and build spiritual unity, for example, at a Sunday Service or Liturgy. *Sung* vocal prayer can be even more effective because it activates both the right and left-brain. Words with music can quickly impress thought content into the unconscious mind and have a powerful effect on a person's life.

Active mental prayer (meditation) is most effective for making change in any human being. By creating images, in meditation, of the way you want to be, you can quickly create a new reality in any area of your life. Active mental prayer is a powerful way to "make things happen."

Passive mental prayer (contemplation) is the most perfect and most mature of all modes of prayer. In contemplation you experience being one with God, Beauty, Truth and Goodness. Passive mental prayer is a state in which you "let things happen." This is the state into which the saints and holy people of all ages eventually arrived. This state is the most perfect state of existence that a human being can enter!

4. Visualization

Trying to describe how the mind knows is a real challenge. In English we have only a few words for this process. We say, for example, the mind "knows," or I "understand," or I'll "think" about it. But none of these terms explain *how* knowing happens.

In order to talk about what we cannot explain, we borrow terms that, we hope, will make it easier. For example, we borrow the term "visualize" from what the eye does, the reason being that the eye sees in much the same way as the mind knows. Suppose you purchase a painting to put on your living room wall. You are so excited about what it does for your room that you get on the phone and try to tell a friend about it. However, no matter how long you are on the phone, the other person will never be able to understand exactly what you mean. Words simply cannot convey the experience of the painting. If you want the other person to get the experience of the painting, you must invite him/her to your home and show the picture. Once the person sees the painting, he/she gets the experience immediately in all its detail. The mind "knows" in much the same way.

A writer, for example, can be walking down the street and the idea of a novel pops into his/her head. The entire thing comes at once in all its detail. However, it may take the author many months to put it all on paper.

Because the mind knows instantly and completely, we say the language of the mind is "images." It is as if there is a "picture" in the mind. These expressions are only ways for us to *try* describing how the mind knows.

Frequently when I am teaching a meditation class, students approach me with comments like these: "When I close my eyes to meditate, I don't see anything," or "All I see is black." My response is always the same, "Do you *understand* when I am taking you through a guided meditation?" Their answers are always, "Yes, of course." Then I tell them, "Whatever you are doing when you say 'I understand' or 'I know what you mean' is what I am referring to when I say 'visualize'." If the word "visualize" is not a good one to describe how you know, then don't use it. The fact of the matter is, anyone who "thinks" or "knows" is doing what we call "visualization."

Here is how visualization would appear in a typical relaxation exercise. Close your eyes, take a deep breath and imagine yourself in a beautiful meadow on a warm summer day. You are seated under a tree, very comfortable and very relaxed. There are mountains in the distance and you can hear the sound of a nearby brook. There are wild flowers everywhere and you can sense their soft, sweet scent. Using these "images" will cause your mind to relax and will sustain relaxation throughout the meditation.

In the meditation itself, you can "picture" your body filled with light, which represents God's presence, healing and love. You can "imagine" light causing your body to glow and to radiate a soft blue-white hue. After that you can "look ahead" into the day to picture the things you want to accomplish, for example, taking the children to school, going to work, shopping, visiting a friend, studying, etc. "See" each of these tasks as completed and successful.

Using your mind in this way during meditation is a powerful way of creating the life you want. If you fill your mind with good, healthy, wholesome, positive images, you will be giving directions to the Mind to create a good, healthy, wholesome, positive life. What you "visualize" in your mind will certainly become a reality in your life!!!

William James applied this process to the definition of "possible." He said: "What the mind can conceive and believe, is possible."

I believe that visualization (creating pictures in the mind) is the *most powerful* way for any person to change anything in life.

5. Time and Frequency of Meditation

For centuries, monastic tradition demanded meditation morning and evening. The Silva class suggests that meditation take place not only morning and evening, but also at mid-day. In my opinion, meditation three times a day is ideal. A morning meditation can help you plan the day, a noon-day meditation can "re-charge" you, and an evening meditation can give you the opportunity to review the success of the day and prepare you for a restful night.

In the monastery, we were taught to meditate for one-half hour each morning and evening. The Silva Method suggests that "5 minutes is good, 10 minutes is very good, and 15 minutes is excellent. Once a day is good, twice a day is very good, and three times a day is excellent." Other systems suggest 15 to 20 minutes.

In rare cases do the experts suggest an hour or more. In our present society, with the busy schedules of most people, I find a maximum of 15 minutes for each session practical and effective.

I might add here that it takes discipline to go into meditation daily, but I also want to stress the discipline of coming out of meditation and then creating results in daily life! Some years ago, after teaching a meditation class, I got a call from a woman who had been in class with her husband. She called to tell me that she had a problem. "My husband is meditating every morning," she explained. "That sounds like a positive to me," I replied. She went on to say, "But Father, when I tell him it's time to got to work he tells me he just wants to continue meditating."

This situation is not uncommon. The feeling that comes from deep relaxation is so pleasant and enjoyable, you may be tempted to stay there longer than 15 minutes. However, I believe that in meditation we get direction to make our lives and world better. But because God can do no more *for* us than what we allow God to do *through* us, we have to discipline ourselves to come out of meditation and get into the business of living. Once we get direction for the day or solutions to problems and challenges, we need to get off our duffs and make it happen!!

6. Place for Meditation

Although you can meditate anywhere, I suggest that if possible you have a designated place specifically set aside for this daily activity. The reason for this suggestion is that if you return to the same place for each meditation, the place itself becomes a cueing mechanism to help you reach the meditation state quickly.

Of course, in a monastic setting we were blessed to have a chapel or choir set aside for that purpose only. But you can find or create such a place in your life, too.

I knew a Jewish gentleman who began and ended each day in a Catholic chapel. The place was conveniently located on his way to work and provided a distinct atmosphere of quiet that made meditation easy and effective.

I also know a woman who created a Japanese garden in her home with flowing water and a meditation stool. This is a designated place of quiet for anyone in the family and respected as such, at all times of the day and night. Even when one of the children misbehaved, he/she could take "sanctuary" on the meditation stool and even the parents had to respect the youngster's quiet (and I might add, helped the parents to "cool down").

This place can be outside in your garden, on a rooftop, in front of a planter, on a beach, in your favorite armchair in the living room, or in a corner of the bedroom. Any place that is secluded and quiet will work. However, always remember, you can meditate anywhere, even on a bus going to work or on a commuter train. In these cases, if you close your eyes and create a "prayer place" in your imagination you will find this "inner place" will work as effectively as an "outer place."

7. Posture for Meditation

When I am teaching meditation I recommend that my students use a straight-back chair (so the back can be well supported), feet flat on the floor, hands on the lap with palms open and facing upward, eyes closed. There are good reasons for this posture.

First of all, posture sends a message to the mind. For example, if you were to lie down on a thickly carpeted floor, close your eyes and begin a relaxation exercise, the message sent to the mind is "Sleep!" More likely than not, you would normally fall asleep in such a situation. However, if you are in an erect sitting position in a straight-back chair as described above, the message given to the mind is "be alert" even though the body is directed to relax.

We suggest that the feet be flat on the floor to aid in proper circulation during the meditation. Crossed legs can cut off circulation and become a distraction.

The position of the hands is also significant. First of all, when you come to meditation, especially after a busy day, you may have a lot of pent-up energy that must be released. Usually, this energy leaves the body through the top of the head, the palms of the hands, and the soles of the feet. For this reason, in the Far East, meditators use the lotus position, which places both the palms of the hands and the soles of the feet in an upward position.

This open-hand position also helps psychologically. Palms turned upward and opened suggest that the person be open to both receiving and giving.

For most people, closed eyes are helpful to keep out distraction. On the other hand, I have found some people who are more relaxed with their eyes open and for them "open eyes" can be more effective. Do what works for you!

It is important to remember that the experienced meditator can meditate anywhere in any position. In the Far East, as well as in the West, meditators sometimes stand on their hands, or walk or stand on one leg or stand on both legs, etc. In the beginning, traditional positions are used for training purposes. After sufficient experience, positions can be altered to suit the needs of the particular person.

For years I have been approached and asked, "What method do you use in your own meditation?" My response has always been, "I use the 'Justin Method'." By that I mean I have taken from all the information I have gathered over the years and shaped my meditative experience in a unique and personal way. I believe that any student of meditation will be most effective when he/she tailors meditation to his/her individual, personal needs and situations. Listen to every teacher, read as much as you can, and then take what is valuable for you and leave the rest. Create your own personalized approach!

8. Conclusion

I think it is important to remember that meditation is one of the most natural processes in the world. All of us know, intuitively, how to meditate, although we may not use that term. For example, we all seek to find quiet in our lives at some time or another. Perhaps it might be sitting on the porch in a swing or a rocker, or at the side of a swimming pool or at the beach, in a park or in the back yard. This need for quiet comes from the unconscious because, at that level, we know we have to realign our "energy" and quiet is the way that happens. Sleep is part of that process, a "sister" to meditation.

Meditation is simply "you becoming aware of the Divine Presence within you, a 'place' where you can get direction for your life, find solutions to problems in your life and where you can come in touch with all that is good, all that is true and all that is beautiful."

It is my hope that as you understand what meditation is and how powerful it can be in your life, you will take the time to develop this natural gift and use it daily to enrich your life – beyond your wildest dreams!

9. Suggested Activities for Chapter III

1. Use the Hermitage Meditation #7 – Basic Relaxation – to experience and practice physical and mental relaxation.

2. Use the Hermitage Meditation #1 – Universal Morning and Evening Meditation - to practice the use of visualization and to practice active meditation.

3. Use the Hermitage Meditation #19 – Learning (made fast and easy) - to apply meditation to study and test taking.

4. Determine a place where you can meditate daily and create there an atmosphere that will help you relax physically and mentally: a comfortable chair, a picture, a candle, a flower, etc.

5. Use the Hermitage Meditation #3 – A Contemplative Morning and Evening Meditation - to practice the experience of passive meditation.

6. Practice paying attention to your dreams. Then learn to use dreams to get direction for your life and/or to solve problems in your life.

IV

PRACTICAL APPLICATIONS FOR MEDITATION

When confronted with something new, many people want to know "What is the practical application?" "What good will it do me?" In this chapter we want to suggest applications that you can use every day. We want you to know how meditation can make a difference in your life.

It is important to note that in this chapter we offer only a few examples. Actually meditation has no limit to its applications. My hope is that as you understand the applications described here, you will develop a "feel" for creating your own personal applications.

Note also that we begin with applying meditation to your self. The reason we move in this direction is this: you have direct control over yourself; you do not have direct control over others. For this reason, when you apply meditation to yourself, you can see results immediately. When dealing with others, you can send them thoughts, but they have free will, just as you do! They will get the ideas you send but they must choose to accept them and act on them.

1. Preliminary Principles

Before we get to the actual techniques, there are some basic, fundamental principles that apply to meditation across the board.

a. Meditation Is for Everyone

Meditation is a tool that anyone can use. Scientists tell us that children are in a meditative state almost all the time, from birth through at least seven or eight years of age. That is one of the reasons they learn so quickly.

I remember the first meditation class we produced for children. Some of them were as young as five or six. The class, when given to adults, usually took four full days to complete, but when we taught children, we discovered they learned so quickly we could complete the class in only two days.

Although children use this state naturally, it is important to note that the elderly can use it also. I remember Martha, who took my class when she was approaching 80 years of age. We got to the point in the program where the students were being taught to control pain. That night when she was getting ready for bed, the bursitis in her left shoulder began to act up. Using the techniques she had learned in class that day, she was able to remove the pain in a matter of a few minutes. When she realized that the pain had disappeared she was so excited she could not get to sleep. She then remembered the technique she had learned for going to sleep and, in a matter of a few more minutes, she put herself to sleep and had a very restful night.

Over a period of 30 years I have had students of every age, every nationality, every ethnic, religious, economic and educational background. All have learned to use meditation to improve their lives.

In our culture, for example, it is common for parents to teach children to control pain by using the "cue" of a kiss. "Let mommy kiss it and the pain will go away." When children skin a knee or incur any minor injury, they go to the parent, ask for a kiss on the injury and the pain does indeed disappear. This kind of programming is effective but it does make the children dependent on the parent.

In our classes, we alter this technique a bit. We teach the children to control pain by simply brushing it away with one hand and saying mentally, "Get away, pain!" Because children have no previous "programming" to contradict this directive, they simply say, "Okay" and proceed to control pain by brushing it away and saying, "Get away, pain!" This approach achieves the same result as a parent kiss but the children are no longer dependent on anyone else for applying the technique.

I must say, however, that frequently those with less education find it easier to learn and to use meditation. When we are teaching adults to control pain by going into meditation and simply brushing it away, they look at us in a strange way and with sarcasm in their voice and say, "Sure!!!" The reason for this reaction is that adults have a completely different "program" in the unconscious that says: "The way to control pain is by means of aspirin or some other medication." It is this kind of "education" that can get in the way of using meditation effectively.

Being in a meditative, or altered, state of consciousness is as natural to human beings as sleep. The problem, as I see it, is that Western society teaches children that Beta (the normal waking state) is the most natural state in which to "be." As they grow into their teens, little by little they learn to live at Beta and seldom, if ever, use Alpha and Theta levels of awareness. Then in adulthood, they have to take formal instruction in a program like Silva Mind Development to do what was natural for them in the first place!!!

My point here is anyone can use meditation to find direction for life, to find solutions to problems in life and to make personal changes in life easily and quickly.

b. Meditation Saves Time

In meditation new information can be impressed on the sub-conscious very quickly. Scientific research in "accelerative learning" has proven that students who use meditation before and after study, can speed up the learning process up to seven times the rate of learning in a traditional classroom.

Let me share a rather dramatic example. I had a high school student who asked if meditation could be applied to athletic ability. "Of course," I said, "meditation can be used for anything!" He then explained that he was a senior on the track team and very much interested in becoming the best cross-country runner in the school! (I didn't know at that time that he was, in fact, the *worst* cross-country runner in the history of the school!!!) However, because he was so dedicated, respectful and interested, the coaches decided to leave him on the team for the final year of his high school career. I spent time showing him how to "see" himself in meditation, running the tracks he was so familiar with, but seeing himself passing everyone, and getting to the finish line first.

In the beginning, there was little improvement because he found it difficult picturing himself passing everyone and getting to the finish line first. However, as he practiced, he was able to mentally "see" himself winning. Once the mental images changed, he began to reach the finish line first. At the end of that season, he was not only the best cross-country runner on the team, he also won the district tournament and went into state competition that year. What he had been trying to do for three years, he was able to accomplish in only one season with the help of meditation.

At this point in history we are being asked to move quickly on many important global issues – cleaning our air and water, creating world peace, becoming aware of ecology issues, global sharing of natural resources, limiting population growth, etc., etc. I have no doubt that, if the resource of meditation is developed and used worldwide, we will solve these issues in record time and bring the planet into an era of sustained peace and prosperity!

c. Cueing Mechanisms

All meditation systems use a cueing mechanism of some kind so that an altered state can be achieved quickly. The image of an ideal place for relaxation is one of these. For example, Maxwell Maltz, in his book "Psycho-Cybernetics," suggests the mental creation of a room in which the meditator can picture him/her self comfortable and relaxed. Jose Silva suggests the image of a laboratory with desk, clock, calendar, tools, medications, etc. St. Theresa of Avila used the image of a castle. It doesn't make any difference what kind of mental environment you picture, as long as you use the *same* image each time. Once you practice with a specific image, you will be able to go into a meditative state easily and quickly any time, anywhere.

Taking two or three deep breaths can also be a "cue" to get into meditation easily and quickly. This is especially true with passive meditation where the entire meditation may be concentration on the breathing only. Concentration on, and/or visual images of breath can be an effective cueing mechanism for entering a meditative state.

Sound can also be helpful for entering meditation. Chanting, or listening to chanting, can get a person to relax and enter an altered state. Scientists tell us that the slow movements of Haydn and Mozart symphonies are very effective aids for getting into meditation and remaining in that relaxed state. Jose Silva created a special "Alpha" sound and combined it with the sound of a metronome. This combination of sounds is also effective in helping people reach and sustain a meditative state.

One of our Franciscan saints, Brother Juniper, who lived in Perugia, Italy, used the Italian word "Dio" (God) as a mantra to reach the state of meditation. He had used this word for so long that saying it once would put him into an altered state. Some of the local children, for their own entertainment, would hide around a corner or in a doorway. When the saint came by they would shout "Dio" and immediately the saint would go into an ecstasy.

You can also program yourself to go into meditation by using *physical* cues. For example, I know of doctors who help people with eating disorders. In an altered state, the patients are told that they will lose the craving to eat by simply pulling their ear lobe three times. When they feel the urge to eat, they simply pull on their ear lobe three times and they lose the desire to eat. Jose Silva created such a cueing mechanism by teaching his students to put together the first two fingers and the thumb of either hand.

To understand how the cueing mechanism works, let me use a comparison. I have visited Niagara Falls several times. Part of the tour is a visit to the electric generators that are activated by the falls. Electricity is generated by this single source and sent to major cities in the area. This power source can be accessed in many different ways. Trams and trains, for example, turn a handle and the vehicles move; lights go on with the flick of a switch; toast is made by pushing down on a lever; heating and air-conditioning units are activated by a thermostat, etc., etc. In all these cases, the energy is the same but the means to "turn it on" is different.

Similarly, a great variety of cueing mechanisms can be used to "turn on" the unlimited energy of the universe, which flows through each of us in meditation. We can then direct that energy to accomplish any number of tasks, e.g., improve memory, alter one's body weight, heal a relationship, clarify a goal, etc., etc. From this central source within each of us, we can heal the body, pick up information at a distance, wake ourselves up, put ourselves to sleep, remember and understand dreams, etc.

Learning how to get into meditation easily and quickly will connect you to an unlimited source of energy that can enrich every area of your life, expand your awareness, and make your life full!

2. Specific Techniques

In this section, we want to describe how you can use meditation for yourself. As we mentioned earlier you have direct control over yourself; you do not have direct control over others. For this reason, as you learn to apply meditation to yourself, you can see results immediately.

Another important thing to remember is this: It is impossible to give you the *experience* of meditation using this book. In my estimation, the best way to learn meditation is with a teacher. If you try to learn from a book and the book begins by saying: "Close your eyes, take a deep breath, and while exhaling allow your body to relax…" how can you continue using the book when your eyes are closed?

In this printed volume, the only thing we can do is explain, suggest and give direction. Perhaps some of the following applications will help you understand the practical use for meditation, but you will have to take the time yourself to do the exercises, and to get the actual experience yourself.

Over the years, the Hermitage has created audio recordings, which can be used effectively for persons wanting to learn meditation. We offer suggestions from these recordings as we go. You can also find a complete list of our published recordings at the end of this volume or on our website: www.FrJustin-Hermitage. org.

a. Wake Yourself Up

For many people in our society waking up in the morning is a difficult, even painful experience. Part of the reason for this is that most of us are taught to wake up with an alarm clock. What frequently happens with this approach is that we are awakened when brain frequencies are very low, either in Alpha or Theta. It is not a pleasant experience to be jarred out of these brain frequency levels by a loud noise.

However, if we learn to use our minds to wake ourselves up each morning, the experience can be much more pleasant. By activating the mind and the brain in the process of awakening, it is possible to adjust the sleep cycle so that we awaken when the brain frequencies are moving up into Beta.

You might want to try using this process so that you can experience for yourself what it feels like. The procedure is simple. At night when you are in bed and before going to sleep, allow your body and mind to relax. (Perhaps you can use the Relaxation Exercise suggested at the end of this book.) When you are fully relaxed, picture in your mind the time that you want to awaken. Actually picture a clock marking the time that you want to wake up. Tell yourself you will awaken at that time. Then simply go to sleep. You will be amazed to find that you awaken at the time you desire and that the waking-up process is pleasant.

If the process does not work for you the first time you use it, don't be discouraged. Practice may be required, but practice makes perfect. I can assure you, when the mechanism begins to work, it will work for the rest of your life. I started using this method years ago and have not used an alarm clock since. I might add that even when I travel across several time zones, this system works.

b. Put Yourself to Sleep

Another practical application of meditation is putting yourself to sleep. Have you ever been in a situation where you cannot fall asleep? I remember when I was helping my cousin move from one house to another. We had only two days to do the entire job in order to make the building available for the new owners. We worked 10 or 12 hours the first day and after we had eaten our evening meal and gotten to bed, all I could think of were the boxes that still had to be moved. I was thinking, "We will have to move the big ones first because we have the use of the truck for only a few hours. The bedrooms have to be set up before the day is over and we still have to have all the boxes in the garage so they can be locked up..." Although my body was exhausted from a full day's work and ready to rest, my mind was going a mile a minute and I just could not fall asleep. It is at a time like this that knowing how to put yourself to sleep is a blessing!

Here again, the process is simple. Get relaxed and into a meditative state. Now direct your thoughts to create an image that will help you sleep. You can, for example, count down form 20 to 1 or from 40 to 1, BUT tell yourself that as you count down, your brain frequencies will slow down and take you into a deep and restful sleep. It may help to use a dramatic image like numbers passing in front of you as you shoot them down; or imagine numbers flashing, in bright red, at the top of a building late at night; or see the numbers on box cars as a train passes quickly before you. The important thing is that you activate your mind and keep it concentrating on the numbers. Whatever technique you choose, be consistent and use the same images all the time. Repetition will make your images an effective cueing mechanism that will work quickly and effectively, as you continue to use them.

I have been teaching meditation over 30 years. During that time I have had insomniacs in my classes wanting to know how to use meditation to overcome their inability to sleep. One case stands out in my mind, because it was the first of my teaching career and quite dramatic.

A gentleman by the name of Joe, and his wife, Yvonne, were in my class for the first time. Joe had not had a full night's sleep in 10 years and his wife had to be inconvenienced by his constant getting up at night. When we came to that part of the meditation class related to sleep control, Joe's attention became acute. That night he used a countdown exercise. He counted from 100 to 1 and began all over again. By the time he counted to 40, he fell asleep and slept until morning! When he came to class the next morning, with his wife, Yvonne wanted to share his success story because she, too, had a good night's sleep!!! I suggested that Joe continue to use the process and to report to us the following week. With practice, it took Joe less and less time to fall asleep, until finally, all he had to do was relax and he would fall asleep and stay asleep until morning.

What struck me so forcefully about this story was that Joe had spent large amounts of money on doctors and medication over a period of ten years, but it took only one experience in meditation to take him into a process that created normal, natural healthy sleep patterns.

c. Overcome Jet Lag

Because I travel a great deal all over the world and have experienced the discomfort of jet lag, I was motivated to use meditation to deal with it. I figured that, if meditation could help me wake up each morning in a pleasant way, and effectively put me to sleep at night, perhaps it could help me to adjust to a change in time zones.

I was leaving for Europe on a flight scheduled out of New York at 6 PM. After we reached cruising altitude, we were served drinks and then dinner. We were then invited to watch a movie. After the movie we had only one hour or so for sleep. In preparation for sleep, I went into meditation and told myself that the time I was going to experience in sleep, would be the normal five hours I usually get each night. (Remember, in meditation there is no limit of time or space.) I went to sleep from meditation. When I awoke an hour or so later, I got up from my seat and went to the restroom. There I washed, brushed my teeth, shaved and did the things I do each morning when I get up. I wanted to reinforce the idea that this is a normal morning and I am feeling as I do when I get up each morning. When I returned to my seat to have breakfast, I was feeling wonderful and when we landed I was able to go through the entire day, as I normally would, and went to sleep that evening at my usual time. I had little discomfort, and the next day my body was on European time and I was feeling great! I was amazed how effective meditation could be for helping me adjust to another time zone with such little effort.

Let me offer you a little bit of advice. When you travel and want to adjust to a different time zone, always set your clock or watch to the local time. Constantly looking at the current time will program your mind to that reality and help you make the adjustment.

Some years ago, I led a pilgrimage to the Holy Land. In the group, were two nuns from Omaha, Nebraska. When I met them in New York and before leaving the country, they made a point of telling me that one of them would be keeping her watch on Omaha time and the other would keep her watch on local time. Needless to say, they had a difficult time adjusting to a new time zone when we arrived in the Middle East.

On the way back to the States, I made arrangements to travel with them to Omaha for a visit with my family. Of course, I used meditation again to adjust to the time change. The Sisters, however, were comparing Jerusalem time, first to European time, then to New York time, etc. I had a most enjoyable return trip, while the Sisters were getting more and more tired. By the time we reached Omaha, the Sisters were exhausted and, I found out later, had needed a few days to adjust to Central Time. On the other hand, I arrived in Omaha feeling energized and went home to visit with my parents for a couple of hours before going to bed. The next morning, my body was on Omaha time.

Using meditation for adjusting to new time zones is a wonderful tool and one that can be valuable for anyone who travels a great deal!

d. Remember Dreams

As a young friar, we were told not to pay attention to dreams because that was "occult." Being an obedient Franciscan, I followed all the directions and did not pay attention to my dreams. Whenever anyone asked if I had a dream, I would back away with my hands in the air and say, "No! No! I don't dream!!" In actual fact, I had systematically taught myself to forget my dreams,

However, when I began studying meditation from a scientific point of view, I had to get involved in the study of dreams. Little by little I began to realize that what I had been taught about dreams in the seminary was all wrong. In fact, during a year of sabbatical, I spent a whole semester in Jerusalem going through the Bible studying all the passages that referred to dreams. It soon became clear to me that God has communicated frequently with individuals through all of recorded history. In both the Old and New Testaments of the Bible, there are numerous accounts of how God gave direction and understanding to many individuals in dreams. More importantly, I realized that God is speaking to all of us in our dreams, every day!

Since that time, I have paid close attention to my dreams and to this very day, use dreams to get direction for my life, find solutions to problems in my life, confirm much of my personal experience, and clarify my beliefs. I know now that dreams are valuable tools by which God speaks to us, often daily!!!

The first step, then, must be to remember dreams. If you do not remember your dreams, I suggest that you begin by simply remembering one dream. Before you go to sleep at night, relax, go into a meditative state, and tell your sub-conscious that you want to remember a dream. Tell yourself that in the morning you will remember that dream. Then go to sleep from meditation.

You will have the dream! The trick is to remember it. To help you remember the dream, put a pad and pencil at your bedside, or a tape recorder. When you awaken during the night after having a dream, do not move any part of your body, not even your eyelids. Remain very still and mentally review the details of the dream (several times if possible). Only after the dream review, take up the pad and pencil and jot down details of the dream (It may be easier, if you have a tape recorder, to speak the details of the dream into a microphone). Once you have recorded the dream, go back to sleep. When you awaken in the morning, you will find that the few details you saved in writing (or recording), will act like hooks that reach down into your sub-conscious to pull up the dream into your conscious awareness.

Here again, if you do not remember dreams at this point in your life, it may take some practice before you can develop this skill. But, IF YOU PRACTICE, I can promise you will soon find it easy to remember your dreams, which you can then use to get direction for your life and/or to solve problems in your life.

e. Heal Yourself

A valuable application of meditation is in the area of healing and promoting health. If you recall, we stated earlier that, if you fill your mind and your brain with good, healthy, wholesome, positive thoughts, you will create a good, healthy, wholesome, positive life. In applying this principle to health and healing, we have the support of science. Psycho-neuro-immunology has proven that the thought process is directly connected to the immune system. The application can be summed up in this statement: Fill your mind with good, healthy, wholesome, positive thoughts and you will turn on the immune system. Fill your mind with evil, sick, base, negative thoughts and you will shut down the immune system.

What we want to do, at this point, is to give you a few suggestions on how you can use the mind and the brain, in the meditative state, to promote health and healing.

i. Get Rid of Headaches

Most headaches are created by stress. When people get stressed, muscles commonly contract. When that happens, pressure is put on the circulatory system, which lessens the flow of blood to the brain. It is the lessening of blood to the brain that causes pain.

The solution is simple. If you go into a meditative state and allow your body to relax, the blood vessels expand so that the blood can flow freely again.

The technique to remove headaches is easy. Go into meditation so that you can relax physically and mentally. While in meditation, picture your muscles completely relaxed and mentally see the blood flowing naturally and normally throughout the body, especially in the brain. Remain in meditation for a few minutes and then slowly open your eyes. You will find that the headache will have disappeared so that you can continue your day pain free.

It is interesting to note that these simple facts and techniques are not exposed to the general public by the medical establishment. Rather, we are told, the way to control headaches is to take some form of medication, and so we have a multimillion-dollar industry creating pills and capsules to solve the problem. The industry is not interested primarily in helping people solve a problem; it is interested in making money. Once people develop the skill of relaxation, and are taught how to apply this skill to headache control, they will stop buying pills. It doesn't cost a lot to learn these skills, but they can enrich our lives, promote health and save money! – On the other hand, these simple techniques can have a devastating effect on the economy of the drug industry!

This technique can also be applied to migraine headaches. Although the cause for migraine discomfort can be entirely different from that for stress headaches, the same approach can be used to solve the problem.

Sometimes when individuals are constantly living under pressure their normal mode of existence is "stress." When they finally do relax, the blood vessels may expand too much and when that happens in the brain, it can cause cluster migraine headaches. The same meditative technique can be used to solve this problem.

If you have a migraine headache, go into a meditative state and allow your body and your mind to relax. Once you are there, mentally picture the blood vessels functioning in a normal, healthy manner. After you have been in meditation for four or five minutes, slowly open your eyes and pay attention to how you feel. If the discomfort has not disappeared completely, wait a few minutes and go into a meditative state again using the same procedure. With migraine headaches, it may be necessary to use two or three sessions to control the situation, but it will work!

I recall an individual who came into my class because she heard that the material could be applied to migraine headaches. She had had this problem for nearly 10 years. She came into my class and was very attentive when we got to the section of the course related to self-healing. The next time she started to feel a migraine coming on, she applied the techniques she had learned in class and was able to control the headache completely. A couple of years later I heard her relating to a class how she learned this skill and now does not have to deal with migraines any more. What is even more interesting were the details she added. She explained that over a ten-year period she had spent over $20,000 on doctor, hospital and medication bills and did not solve the problem. It was only after one meditation session that she was able to control the migraines completely.

ii. Get Rid of Pain

It is possible to apply meditation to any life situation, especially areas of health and healing. Taking control of and overcoming pain is part of that process.

In the same way that you can apply meditation to removing a headache, so you can use this state to overcome any pain. The process once again is very simple.

When you experience any discomfort, simply go into meditation, picture the pain as color or liquid (or any other image) and then mentally see it disappear or flow out of the body. When I was younger, I used to run every day. Sometimes it would be too soon after lunch and while running I would get a pain in my side. I would simply allow my hand to brush against my body where I felt the pain and mentally say, "Get away, pain!" I would picture it like a liquid working its way to the surface of the skin and there I would brush it away. Always, in a matter of a few minutes, the pain disappeared completely.

This process, as I said previously, can be taught to small children, even those under the age of seven. Once children personally experience the effect, they are able to use the process for the rest of their lives.

A bit of a caution is in place here. Pain is a natural sign given by the body to indicate that something is not right. Therefore, if a pain recurs, it is appropriate to see a physician or healthcare practitioner.

I think it is valuable, at this point, to recall that the Divine Energy we contact in meditation is the cause for all the effects experienced in this state. God is present with us all the time. Meditation is simply our becoming aware of that Presence and giving It direction.

It is good to recall also that God cannot do anything more for us than what we allow God to do through us. That means we must *choose* to direct our thought process in a given direction or make a choice to *engage* this Unlimited Energy in a specific way. Only then can the Power flow.

I believe that God wants for us to be healthy and happy. For that reason, I believe we all are vested with the same Divine Power that was given to Jesus, to Buddha, to the saints and to the holy people of all major religions. Jesus said, "Those who believe in me will do what I do. Yes they will do even greater things..." (John 14:12). It is up to each of us to activate this energy by conscious intention.

iii. Stop Bleeding

Joe, a former high-school student of mine, was in the armed forces serving in the Far East. He knew that I was interested and involved in meditation and the study of psychic and mystic experience. He related this story to me with great enthusiasm.

One of his buddies had been hit by a piece of shrapnel and an artery in his leg had been cut. A medic came to him to offer assistance but the wounded soldier pushed the medic aside and told him to get to other men who had been wounded because he could take care of himself. The medic told the soldier that he had to have a tourniquet on this leg or he would bleed to death. The soldier insisted that he could take care of himself and pushed the medic away. In frustration, the medic hurried to another wounded soldier and fully expected the first soldier to bleed to death.

A few days later the medic was making rounds in the hospital and to his amazement found the first soldier in bed recovering from his wound. He approached the bed, asked how the soldier was doing and told him that he fully expected him to bleed to death on the field. The soldier explained that he had taken the Silva Meditation Course and had learned how to control bleeding. The medic refused to believe him. Then the soldier said, "Here, I'll show you." He reached to the side of his bed, took a razor blade and cut his fingertip. "Look," he said, "my finger is bleeding." Then he closed his eyes, took a deep breath and in a meditative state brushed his hand over the finger-wound while he visualized the blood flow stopping. In a matter of seconds the bleeding stopped and the medic was dumbfounded. "I told you I could take care of myself," said the soldier.

After Joe related the story to me, he expected me to be surprised. I told him that I had been trained to teach the Silva Method of Meditation, and that I was teaching those very techniques. Would you believe, Joe was in my next class!

Parents who have been in my classes teach these techniques to their children. Once they know the process, they can stop bleeding by merely brushing a wound and mentally say, "Get away, blood!"

The explanation of these situations is found in the power of the meditative state. By going into meditation, where there are no limits of time or space, and picturing what it is that you desire, you can cause the brain to direct the body to specific and virtually unlimited results.

None of what I write is "magic," nor is it a "miracle." It is simply the application of laws that until now have not been common knowledge. These laws are being understood and applied by more and more health practitioners and as time goes on will be applied universally.

St. Augustine said that there is no such thing as a miracle. There is only the application of laws about which we know little or nothing.

When children are taught to work with computers from the first grade on, they become near professionals by age 13 or 14. Imagine what it will be like when meditation skills are taught to children from their earliest years. By the time they become teenagers, they will be able to control pain and bleeding without any difficulty. With the use of meditation, they will also be able to promote health and overcome illness!!

f. Improve Memory

Learning to use mind in new and creative ways can help improve memory. Bruno Furst did the original research and published a book describing techniques that can help a person remember names, faces, lists of objects, significant dates, events, numbers, etc.

When teaching a meditation class, I include an exercise, from Bruno Furst's material, to show students how they can remember 90 items. This exercise takes only about a half-hour. The idea is to relate a number to a peg word, which in turn can be associated with an object. It is a simple but effective process.

I know a high school history professor who teaches this technique to his students. With this tool, the students can remember events and dates very easily. The result is that these students achieve high scores on all their tests!

When I was teaching in Israel, I had a priest in the class who was studying scripture. He paid little attention to the memory section of my class because he didn't see any practical application for himself at that time. Not too long afterwards, he was facing an exam in which he had to memorize the content of St. John's Gospel. Scanning his memory for any means to help him deal with this challenge, he remembered the memory pegs of the meditation class. He applied the process to the Gospel of John and was able to remember the major headings of the book in correct sequence. This task took him only 20 minutes and on his exam he got a perfect score. Needless to say, he was grateful to have learned this technique for activating memory!!

g. Create, Control, or Change Habits

Habits are an essential part of our lives. They are a way for us to process huge amounts of information so that our lives can be more enjoyable, more efficient and more effective.

Habits can be explained as programming information into the unconscious. Take for example the process by which a child learns to walk. When held by the hands in an upright position by a parent, the baby records that experience on the brain. Seeing people walking is also recorded on the brain. After a time, the child learns to lean on objects to maintain an upright position. Eventually he/she learns to stand without any support. Trying to take a first step, the baby falls. All of these experiences are recorded on the brain and stored in the unconscious. At some point, the child learns to walk.

All of us had to learn the skill of walking the same way and as we continue to mature we continue to store every experience of walking. We are now so efficient that if we step on an uneven surface, we can process hundreds, even thousands of pieces of information in a second or two, adjust our bodies differently and avoid falling.

This same process applies to language. First we learn words that are repeated for us over and over again. Then we learn phrases and eventually we can communicate. We get so proficient that we can concentrate on ideas and out of the unconscious come all the words we need to communicate our ideas. And so it is for habits of typing, dancing, skiing, eating, etc.

The problem arises when a habit becomes obsolete or counter-productive. Children, for example, get into the habit of going to parents for their every need. As they get older, they have to mature. Part of that process is changing the habit of being dependent on parents and beginning to be dependent on themselves. It is not always easy to make these changes, but if they are to mature, the change must happen. Knowing how to use the mind can make the process easier and speed up the change.

Suppose a child develops the habit of eating certain foods, which are good for growth and physical development. But as the child matures these habits may become counter-productive, especially if the child's metabolism slows down. Foods that were good for him/her at a previous time may become detrimental. The child must therefore alter habits.

Let me use an example. I had a gentleman in one of my classes by the name of John. He came to the class because he wanted to get back to his ideal weight, 160 lbs. In order to reach that goal he had to get rid of 25 lbs. Applying what he learned in class, he went into meditation daily and pictured himself at this ideal weight. He visualized that goal by seeing himself stepping on a scale, seeing the scale read 160, and looking at a wall calendar which identified the date on which he wanted to reach his goal.

When he began this program he was a very sedentary individual. His work demanded that he be seated all day and he did not get involved in much physical exercise. As he began to use meditation he developed a desire to help straighten out the shop every day at noon. So, instead of taking a nap or playing cards with other employees, he began to clean up the shop, putting things in order and doing other physical activity. Little by little, he added enough exercise to his daily schedule that he began to lose weight without changing any of his eating habits. It did happen that on the day he visualized, he stepped on the scale and weighed in at his ideal weight.

John's habit of living a very sedentary life without much exercise was working against him, in terms of his health. By using meditation, he was able to change that habit to one that not only helped him become healthy, but also helped him to continue to be healthy.

Please remember the principle: what a human being can picture in his/her mind, and believe, is possible. If you will take the time to learn the discipline of meditation or mental prayer, and picture in your mind what you desire, you can change any habit in your life.

3. Conclusion

The purpose of this chapter is to show you how you can use meditation to take control of your life. Remember, you can control yourself, because you can control how you think.

Please remember, the suggestions in this chapter are only sample applications. There are unlimited ways to use meditation to make your life full and rich. The question now is: will you take the time to learn how to meditate and then discipline yourself to use this skill daily?

4. Suggested Activities for Chapter IV

1. Before you go to sleep tonight, picture the time you want to wake up in the morning. Use your mind instead of an alarm clock.

2. Before you go to sleep tonight, tell yourself that you will remember a dream. Share the dream with someone the next day.

3. Next time you have a headache, get rid of it by using meditation.

4. Think of a habit that you would like to change or create. Use meditation to make the change.

5. If you have not had a class in meditation, find out if there is one in your area and book a seat in the next class.

V

UNIVERSAL SPIRITUALITY

The title of this book implies that you are successful as a human being when you develop "full thinking." The logic is, if you think "full," it is only a matter of time until your *life* is "full." The thoughts must come first! They are the cause that produces the effect.

This chapter is to challenge you to think universally, seeing all creation as a magnificent unit, of which we are all a part and into which we must place ourselves in relation to the whole. It is this kind of thinking, I believe, that is the mind of Jesus, Buddha, Krishna, and all the great spiritual leaders of the world

Native Americans had this kind of universal thought process. They wanted to live in harmony with nature and strove to "fit into" the whole scheme of things. I remember a story I read years ago. A group of Native Americans wanted to make a journey. They soon realized that their route would take them through a forest that was foreign to them. Before they ventured into the area, they camped and in meditation asked the plants and animals of the forest for permission to pass through. They waited until it was clear that permission had been granted. During their sojourn in that forest, not so much as a mosquito attacked them.

In the past, thinking of the Western world has been completely different. We have considered human beings as the highest form of creation AND in control of everything. This idea implies that humans can do as they please without thinking of the whole. Most of us know where this thought process has led us: enormous ecological challenges, destruction of whole cultures, a preoccupation with money, a struggle for power, a growing separation between rich and poor, and a disregard for the spiritual dimension of reality.

At this time in history, there is more and more interest in a universal spirituality that will bring balance into our world, a thought process that will help us clean up the planet, and a movement to create family relationships among all human beings around the globe.

In this chapter we will discuss a spirituality that considers equal relationships with things, plants, animals, human beings, ourselves and with spirit.

1. Our Relationship with Things

In Western society, there is a great deal of interest and concern for acquiring and possessing material things. Sometimes "success" is measured only by the amount of money and/or possessions a person has. In fact, people with money and possessions are identified as people of power.

In my way of thinking, "success" is not money. Rather, I believe that "success" is living life to the "full" (as described in my previous book, "Success: Full Living"). I believe that a successful human being is one who has balance in every area of life, eager to share whatever he/she has and who loves and accepts people as they are, where they are. This approach has little to do with how much a person possesses in terms of money and/or material things.

I am a follower of St. Francis of Assisi, who lived in the early 1200s. After experiencing the affluence of his father and the power of being a knight, Francis listened to the Divine Voice within his heart and chose to live a life with very few possessions.

Zefferelli, in his famous film on St. Francis, "Brother Sun, Sister Moon," beautifully captured an important moment in the saint's life. Peter Bernadone, Francis' father, drags him to the house of the Bishop. All of the townsfolk are gathered in the square and Mr. Bernadone accuses his son of giving away his goods and his money. He then demands restitution.

When asked to explain himself, Francis tells the Bishop that he simply wants to follow Christ, who had few things and who was free like the birds. Francis then takes off his shirt, his shoes and his trousers. He carries them to his father and says: "Father, I give back all that is yours, including your name. Up to now, I have called you, Peter Bernadone, my father. But from now on, I will say, 'Our Father, who art in heaven.'"

As Francis stands in the middle of the square naked, the Bishop becomes embarrassed, takes off his own cape and tells his assistants "Cover him up!" But Francis cannot accept such a lavish piece of clothing and gives it to a beggar. In return, Francis receives a beggar's cloak, for which he is grateful and leaves the town to start his new life of utter simplicity.

From then on, Francis lived in great joy with few things; wanting to do nothing more than live the way Jesus lived. Financially, according to present day standards, Francis would be considered a total failure. On the other hand, he was the person who, single-handedly, changed the course of European history, and who was a strong and powerful leader.

My point is this: Francis had the courage to follow his heart and to put material things into their proper perspective. He did not despise material things; he simply lived with what he needed and got to the business of living his life, as he felt called to live it! Francis is not the only person who saw the power in living simply. Gandhi, Buddha, and Mother Teresa all embraced a similar life style and became very successful and powerful *human beings.*

I, too, believe in living with few material things and sharing any excess with others. Over the years, I have generated a great deal of income from my work and publications but have kept none of it for myself. What income I create goes to the Franciscan Order or to the Center where I work. My only concern is to help people find their way in this life and to help them come in touch with others who think the way they do and who can give them support on their life journey.

During all my life, I have found it interesting to watch people collecting things. They fill drawers and closets, basements and attics, then the garage. Now businesses provide storage spaces where "stuff" can be stored when there is no more room at home!!!

Yard and garage sales, I think, are signs of changing times. They are means of getting rid of excess material baggage and helping people create a feeling of freedom. They are the means, by which, many individuals stay in charge of their possessions so that the possessions do not take charge of them!

Some years ago I read a very interesting book about collecting material things. Don Aslett titled it "Clutter's Last Stand". In it he asked some interesting questions: Do you store plastic bags in plastic bags and put them all in a larger plastic bag? Do you have so many paper bags from the supermarket between your refrigerator and the wall that not even the mice can get through? It is a very humorous book, but it invites the reader to look at his/her relationship to material things and the value of getting rid of what is not needed. The point of the book is that people who get rid of clutter feel a sense of freedom knowing that they are in charge of the things they possess and do not let the things possess them!

I was so impressed with this book that I wrote a poem titled "Ode to Junk" *(see Appendix 1)*. It was published in the Hermitage newsletter and later I got letters from people all over the world. They told me how good they felt after getting rid of several garbage bags of junk. How proud they were after clearing out a closet that hadn't been touched in years. How happy they were giving away good, even unused, clothing they had stored in the attic for years.

I am pleased to see that individuals are becoming professional in this field. Just recently, a friend told me how she hired a person who helped her move from the home she had lived in for 40 years. She didn't know how to begin sifting through all the things she had collected over the years. The professional not only helped her decide what she needed for a two-bedroom condo, but helped her place what she needed in her new home. My friend is a very happy person in her more simple and uncluttered living space!!!

Another point for consideration is ecology. Recycling is a wonderful way of disposing of waste that can be reused. This process not only helps the person getting rid of the clutter, but it also helps society!

I once heard the principle: "If you don't use it over the period of 6 months, get rid of it!" Unused clothing, for example, can either be sold or given to companies that resell to individuals who could not otherwise afford to buy these items. In this case too, everyone wins – those who get rid of the clutter, those who make a living processing it, and those who are able to purchase and use it.

Some years ago I read an article that appeared on the front page of the *Wall Street Journal.* A very wealthy real estate man came home one day to tell his wife that they had made another million dollars. During a discussion that followed, they both agreed they would never be able to use all the wealth they had acquired and began to think of ways to better use what they had saved. They finally agreed to take $73 million of their earnings and put it into a foundation that would help people in developing countries start their own businesses. They agreed that it would be better to live in a more modest home and subsequently moved out of a mansion into a four-bedroom home so they would still have space to guest their children. The husband then decided to carry the idea of simplifying to other wealthy people and traveled the country seeking to build the foundation he and his wife began.

Ten years later, I happened to be watching a documentary on TV. The story was about a young man in India who was a tailor. He wanted to start his own business but did not have the money. He was able to borrow $500, interest free, from the foundation mentioned above. After only a few years, he has his own shop and now employs several other people also. Foundation money continues to help people all over the world!

Especially here in the United States, where we have been so blessed, I believe we need to see the value of living with what we need and not with what we want. So much is wasted in this country while people in other countries go without basics like food and clothing.

In my bedroom-office, I have a set of shelves that helps me process material things. I call it my "gift shelf". When people give me items to express their love, friendship or concern, I am well aware that the material object is only a symbol. The real gift is the love or friendship or concern. These mementos I put on my gift shelf and when someone in my life is celebrating a birthday or anniversary or any other occasion, I frequently go shopping at my gift shelf. I check out what may be meaningful for that particular person, wrap it, and give it away. I figure, "Why not let this symbol give joy to another person?"

I must warn you, however; be careful what you give to whom! Once I was at my gift shelf searching for a birthday gift and found what I thought would be the perfect gift. It was a beautiful bust of St. Francis, who was greatly admired by the person having the birthday. I wrapped it carefully and was excited when she opened it. When her face lit up and her mouth opened, I was pleased. But then she turned to me and said: "Justin, this is the piece I gave you for your birthday last year!" Thinking quickly, I told her I knew she would like it and that she could have it back to enjoy as I did. The following Christmas, that gift was carefully wrapped and given back to me! It is still being passed on again and again to the joy of us both!

The principle applied here is, the real gift is not something material, which means that I can hang on to the real gift forever without being tied down to the symbol. That is not to say we ought to discard all symbols. I do have things, for example, that remind me of loved ones who have died or people and places I have encountered in my travels. These I treasure and keep on the wall or on a shelf, so that I can see them daily and keep important memories alive. Many, many more pictures I have put into albums or given to family or to our archives so that I do not have clutter.

In my private life, I treasure a simple approach. I believe in the ideals, "Small is beautiful" and "Less is better." I have freely chosen to have only one suit, one habit, one winter coat, one winter jacket, a few summer shirts, a few winter shirts and enough underwear for a week. Not that I think this approach is an ideal for anyone else. It is, however, something that works for me and helps me be mobile, happy and free!

Just a couple of days ago, I heard a radio report on the difference between American and Japanese economic systems. The author spoke about the importance of the bottom line in American economy. Above everything else, there must be a profit. As a result, large conglomerates do not give consideration to the small shop owners who are forced out of business by their presence. On the other hand, in Japan, large businesses must limit their growth in order to protect the "Ma and Pa" businesses. The latter system is not as economically efficient as what we have in the USA but it does keep a balance in terms of people and profit.

My question to you, the reader, is what is your relationship with the things you possess? Are you in charge of the relationship or are you addicted? Do you live with what you need or are you busy collecting what you want? Would you be happier and more contented with less?

There is no doubt in my mind that, at this time in history, we must think of living more simply if we want to develop a balanced society that is healthy and happy. There is already a strong movement in this direction that began with the publication of the book "Voluntary Simplicity" by Duane Elgin. More has been written since and all of it has had a positive and supportive influence in my life and in the lives of a great many other people. Perhaps this is an area of your life you would like to explore?

Some suggestions for taking control of your material possessions:

1. Determine how many suits you need. When you buy a new one, give away an old one.

2. When you stay at a hotel, use only one bath towel. Not only will you save the maid some work but you can save the resources that would have to be used to clean the rest of the towels.

3. Use mugs instead of paper or Styrofoam cups so that you can minimize trash.

4. Determine how many shoes you need and give away the rest.

5. Do you have dishes you never use? Determine what you need and give away the rest.

6. Do you have enough linen to stock a shop? Determine what you need and give away the rest.

7. Take a shopping bag with you to the supermarket so that you don't have to use their bags.

8. Clean out your garage, or basement, or attic and then pay attention to how you feel when you get rid of the excess "baggage."

2. Our Relationship with Plants

In the order of nature, we go up the scale from inanimate matter (things) to plant life. This dimension of reality is important for all of us, since plant life is basic in the food chain and one of the foundations on which all life rests. I think it is important for us to look carefully at our relationship with this part of creation, too.

Before being involved in teaching meditation, I had given little thought to this dimension of my life. One summer, while attending an international convention, I had the pleasure of meeting and working with Cleve Baxter. He had been doing plant research for many years and opened my eyes to some very important realities. In one of his lectures, he described how his work began.

By profession, Baxter worked with the polygraph and one day while in his office he was looking at a plant he had near his desk and wondered what would happen if he put the electrodes of the polygraph on the plant. He put one electrode on top of a leaf and another on the bottom of the same leaf and clamped them together. To his amazement, he got a reading that was similar to what he had gotten when he put the electrodes on the skin of a person taking a lie-detector test.

One day, while he had the plant attached to the polygraph, he wondered if he could evoke in the plant what humans experience as emotion. When he thought; "I'll light a match and burn the leaf" he noticed that the electronic readout immediately produced a noticeable reaction. The plant, it seemed, was picking up on Baxter's thought process. This event started a whole new direction to his work and eventually he was able to prove that plants have what he calls, "primary perception."

Some of his experiments were very interesting. At one point he wanted to see if plants had memory. Working with several of his students, he devised an experiment. On a piece of paper, he put directions on how to uproot, stomp on, and destroy one of two plants in a particular room. The paper was placed in a hat with similar pieces of paper that were blank. Several of his students drew from the hat but told no one what they had drawn. The person who drew the directions was to follow them to the letter but at a time when no one could see who did the deed. One plant would be destroyed and the other would be the witness.

When the one plant had been destroyed, Baxter attached the polygraph to the surviving plant in a room all by itself. One by one, the students entered the room and Baxter monitored the polygraph. There was no "reaction" by the plant until the person who had committed the "crime" appeared in the room. When this student was in the presence of the plant, the polygraph's reaction was violent. The plant actually identified the criminal.

Baxter has conducted many other experiments that have caused the biological community of the world to take notice. He showed, for example, that plants can pick up on their caretaker's thought process, even at a distance.

I am sure you are aware of the way some humans can communicate with plants. We sometimes use the term "green thumb" to indicate those who are successful in working with plants. These are people who touch the leaves of plants, talk to them, play music for them, etc. and the plants respond by growing and becoming very beautiful.

Baxter has also proved that plants have personalities as animals do and bond with their caretakers as animals do.

Plants can even communicate with other plants! I read through some of the research done in this area and it is interesting to say the least. One such project discovered that when a tree is attacked by a certain insect, it is able to communicate somehow with the trees in the vicinity. The other trees then begin to produce an acid of some kind that does not harm the tree, but which keeps the insects from attacking them.

All of the above is not just accident or coincidence. The educational community is helping high school biology students to experience these realities firsthand. Students, for example, are asked to take plant seeds and put them into two small containers of water. Both containers receive the same conditions of light and heat, but they are treated differently by the student. The student is told to give a lot of attention to one set of seeds and to ignore the other set. Sometimes the students play music for the seeds, sometimes they talk to them; sometimes they just spend time with the seeds. In every case, the seeds that are given the attention sprout and grow faster than the seeds that do not get the human attention. This kind of experiment can be done by anyone and it will produce the same results again and again.

The Finhorn community in Scotland proved how effective human communication can be with plants. When the community first began, the local people told them that it would be impossible to grow food on that piece of land, at least not enough to feed the entire community. The community planted a garden anyway, but every day the community would circle the garden and in meditation ask the plants to produce what they would need to survive. When the plants began to produce fruit, not only did they produce enough for the community, but there was a surplus that was sold to the local residents. The community did indeed survive because the plants responded to the requests made by those who planted and tended the garden.

Since plants do have perception, it makes sense to learn to communicate with them for our own benefit. Before eating, for example, it is valuable to connect with the plants mentally. Thank the plants for being your food and ask that when they enter your body, they give you health and strength. This approach to making a mental connection is nothing more than another approach to traditional prayer before meals. You simply make a conscious connection between the Divine in the plants and the Divine in you!

Plants, of course, are necessary for our survival. We need oxygen and the plants produce it for us. For that reason we need to respect plant life and allow it to thrive if we are to survive!

I remember Arbor Day from when I was a child in Omaha, Nebraska. It was a holiday throughout the state; a time when people were off work and out planting trees everywhere. That is why the older sections of the city are known for their beautiful wooded lanes and parks. The importance of Arbor Day has become national and the Arbor Day Foundation is responsible for promoting interest and concern for plant life throughout the country and the world.

I am sure that I was no more than three or four years old when my mother showed us how to plant tulip bulbs, morning glory seeds and gladiola bulbs. I can remember watching the cotyledon of a morning glory seed breaking through the ground for the first time and how excited I was watching it grow and mature into a beautiful wall of blue blossoms! Do you know, I still get that same excited feeling today when I put wild flower seeds into the ground and still enjoy watching them grow and blossom!

A few years ago, I was visiting my cousin who had a beautiful bed of daisies next to her kitchen door. When I commented on them, she explained that they had come from my Aunt Irene's flowerbed. Aunt Irene was a lover of flowers and had one of the most beautiful gardens in the neighborhood. She enjoyed cutting the flowers all summer and keeping them in the house. I asked about getting a few of the plants for our Friary in Indianapolis, and carried back only 3 small plants. Now we have a full bed of daisies at our front door that reminds me of my cousin, my aunt and my Creator!!!

Because of personal experiences like these, we have started a memorial program at the Hermitage. When you come to visit you will find many plants, trees and flowers that are a living reminder of family members, friends and benefactors.

As I reflect on these personal experiences, I can understand why planting and caring for plants is so life giving. I remember reading an article about a person in prison ministry who interested authorities in experimenting with a "plant program" for prisoners. Although skeptical at first, the warden allowed the program and was amazed at the personality changes that began to take place in the lives of prisoners who cared for plants. If only we could get these kinds of programs in similar institutions across the country and around the world. Perhaps then we could give plants the opportunity to work their healing magic on so many who need it!!!

Some suggestions for developing a better relationship with plants:

1. Get a copy of "The Secret Life of Plants" by Peter Tompkins and Christopher Bird and educate yourself a bit more about plant life and primary perception.

2. Share a planting experience with your child, grandchild or student and teach them about the mystery of plant life.

3. Purchase a flowering plant for someone who needs to be cheered up but before giving it away, ask the plant to flower generously in order to cheer up your friend.

4. Make a point of mentally connecting with the living food on your table before eating. (Get into the habit of saying "Thanks" before all your meals!).

5. Try an experiment with two seeds or two plants. Give them both the same light, temperature, etc but give a lot of attention to one and ignore the other. See what kind of results you get.

3. Our Relationship with Animals

There are many dimensions of reality to which we humans are connected in the universe. We have already discussed our relationship with things and with plants. Let us now take some time to examine how we are connected with the animal kingdom.

In the same way that plants offer themselves to sustain, beautify and enrich our lives, so, too, do animals offer themselves to sustain, beautify and enrich our lives.

One relationship between animals and humans is also the food chain. All over the planet on a daily basis animals are killed so that humans can sustain their lives. This is a natural process, but sometimes, in the process of killing, the relationship between the animal and we humans is not always healthy.

As a youngster living in Omaha, Nebraska, I was aware that the city was a center for the cattle industry boasting the largest stockyards and slaughterhouses in the world. When guests came from out of town, this was one of the sights on the city tour. I recall one visit when we were watching the steers being killed. They were lined up in a cattle chute and directed under a platform. On top of the platform was a man with a sledgehammer. When the steer passed through the chute below, it was the job of the man above to hit the steer in the center of the forehead, which would cause instant death. However, sometimes the blow was not accurate and the beast would be wounded, not killed. At that point, the animal would moan and struggle while huge amounts of adrenaline began pumping through its system. When this happened, the animals behind would become visibly disturbed also. Although this approach to killing was meant to be humane, when it didn't work properly, it was not a pleasant sight. The trauma of the steer was awful!

On the other hand, according to Jewish custom, when an animal is slaughtered, a very different relationship is prescribed. Jewish law demands that a Rabbi be present to pray over the animal. The procedure requires that the jugular vein be cut so that the animal can die quietly and without trauma. This is one of the reasons why kosher meat can be better tasting and have a better texture.

It was Dr. Gina Cerminara, the author of Edgar Cayce's biography, who first got me interested in problems connected with the animal industry. We were both attending a reincarnation conference in Kingfisher, Oklahoma, and happened to meet at lunchtime one day. She shared with me an experience she had visiting a chicken farm and how appalled she was at the way the animals were treated. She then described how four hens were confined to a very small cage with little or no room for exercise or freedom of movement. When one of the birds attacked another, the farmers would remove the claws and sometimes even the beaks so they could not harm one another.

Dr. Cerminara began to explain how the living conditions had a negative effect on the birds and affected the taste and quality of the meat. But that was not all. She was concerned about the psychological "program" recorded on the cells of these animals so that when eaten as food, the disturbing program would be picked up by the consumer. At that point, I was thinking to myself: If plants have perception and memory, surely these animals do too; and if the memory is stored in the animals' cells, and we consume the cells, it makes sense that we would pick up the program contained in those cells.

In the same way that a dying, wounded steer pumping large amounts of adrenaline into its body as it dies, can transfer that adrenaline to the consumer, cannot the information of a traumatic life recorded in the cells of a hen be transferred to the consumer also? Perhaps this may account for some of the hyperactivity we are seeing today in children, as well as in adults!

Since my encounter with Dr. Cerminara, I look for Amish chickens in the supermarket or those labeled "range farm" because I know they have been treated well and the cellular program is much more positive, not to mention the better quality of the meat and eggs produced by these birds. I have also developed a respect for the Jewish community who continue to produce kosher meats.

Unfortunately, some who are involved in raising and slaughtering animals for food can be so focused on profit that they give little, if any, consideration to the ethics involved, or the responsibility they have to the animals themselves. As I mentioned in my previous book, "Success: Full Living," I think there is a need to balance these different areas of life, if our lives are to be truly full!

As consumers, we have a responsibility to call producers to accountability. By choosing to purchase only those products that have been produced in a humane way, we encourage producers to use proper means of caring for and slaughtering animals. If we don't do our part, we will be just as guilty as those who actually do the injustice.

As a follower of St. Francis of Assisi and a lover of animals, I hope that some of these issues will continue to be social and political ones also. If you and I examine *our* relationship with money, and balance that with our relationship with life, all life, we can make a difference.

I know of rehabilitation programs in prisons and houses of correction where inmates can learn to be kind, gentle, and loving by taking care of an animal. I have seen the lives of older people brighten up when a loving dog or cat is brought into their lives. Now we are seeing animals coming into hospitals and nursing homes, to help patients heal faster and improve their psychological and emotional states.

Here in Indianapolis, there is a group of pet owners whose animals are certified to be part of a pet therapy program at several hospitals in the city. I was invited one day to join them as they visited patients. The first person we visited was a young man who has been completely paralyzed for over 20 years. When a pet dog put its paws on the bed in front of his face, a broad smile appeared on his lips and his entire person lit up. Then a cat jumped onto the bed, spent time directly in front of the young man's face and finally found a snuggling place next to one of his legs. It was amazing to see the change take place in the person of the patient!

Animals can teach us a lot about love and friendship. I remember seeing a documentary about a pig that had bonded with a young goat on a farm. One night the barn caught fire and these two animals were in danger of losing their lives. The pig found a weak spot in the barn wall and broke through it so that both of them could run to safety.

Even more exciting to me are the studies that are being made with dolphins. I have a friend whose daughter does dolphin therapy in Florida. She told me of a dyslexic child who made vast improvement because of contact and communication with dolphins.

I think it wonderful that there is an entire TV channel dedicated to animals. It carries not only information about animals, but also stories and documentaries on how animals enrich our lives and in some cases, how they actually save human lives.

When I am teaching meditation classes, I give suggestions on how we all can communicate with the animal world. As an example, I talk about a student of mine who moved from Ohio to Houston. He was told that he would have to live with cockroaches because they are part of the terrain. However, because he had a great aversion for cockroaches, decided he would do something about it. Before moving anything into the apartment, he went into meditation and mentally contacted all the cockroaches in the vicinity. He told them he loved them but he wanted to warn them. He would allow them to live wherever they needed but were not to show themselves if they valued their lives. The result was that he simply does not see these creatures in his living space. The bugs, I am sure, are happy with the arrangement, as is he!!!

With the expanding awareness of human/animal connections, whole systems of training are being developed. As far back at 1970, Russian animal trainers were developing new and innovative ways of using direct thought process to communicate with animals. In the book "Psychic Discoveries behind the Iron Curtain," the author describes how trainers held the head of a dog between their hands, closed their eyes and pictured the dog jumping through a hoop. When they let the dog go, it immediately jumped through the hoop.

These kinds of gentle, but effective, methods of communication have since moved into other areas of animal training as portrayed in the film "The Horse Whisperer."

Our world will be a better place when all of us have a better relationship with the animal kingdom. How can you improve your relationship with this dimension of creation?

Some suggestions for helping you in this area:

1. If you have a pet, practice mental communication and look for results.

2. Spend some quiet time in a park, in your backyard or any other place where you can observe wild life. Connect mentally with a chipmunk, a bird, a squirrel, a dog or a cat. Note any results.

3. Before eating meat, fish, or even eggs or cheese, thank the animals involved and mentally send them your love.

4. Are you bothered by insects or bugs? Connect with them mentally and ask them to leave you alone. Let them know you respect their lives.

5. Check in the supermarket for Amish or Kosher chickens or cheeses. Compare the quality with other brands.

6. If you have a pet that has graduated from obedience school, check to see if there is an animal therapy program at a local hospital, nursing home or day care center. If none are available, perhaps you can educate authorities to get one started.

7. Pay attention to the number of animals that touch your life each day. Thank them for being there and send them your love.

4. Our Relationship with Human Beings

Having looked briefly at how we can relate to things, plants, and animals, let us take some time to consider our relationship with human beings.

I had the good fortune to be born and raised in a neighborhood where everyone knew everyone else. It was a tightly woven community, created around the church and in which there were common values, mutual love and concern, as well as joy, happiness, and lots of fun.

From our earliest years, my parents taught us to respect the elderly and showed us how to give our time to them. As a result, I had a wonderful rapport with many older people from my earliest childhood. Even as a teenager, I enjoyed driving elderly to the cemetery for a visit, sharing Mass with them on Saturday mornings, dancing with them at weddings, working with them in the kitchen or at the church and always listening to the interesting stories from their earlier lives. What richness I gained from these experts in the art of living!

It saddens me to see children separated, these days, from adults. For example, when I visit a family for dinner or go to someone's house for a party. Most often, the children are in another room or they eat before guests arrive. Not only do I miss the enthusiasm of these young people, but I think of the insight and learning that they could get from listening to conversation of adults.

When I am teaching adults, I often remind grandparents and the elderly what a valuable opportunity they have when they can share with young people. It may not be as easy today as it was when I was a child, but with a bit of ingenuity, it can happen.

Not long ago I was directing a Retreat at Sea. We got on this topic of relationships between young and old. One of the women in the group had been telling wonderful stories about her life, her children, etc. Unfortunately her children were living in many different parts of the country and it was difficult for her as a grandparent to get time with them and the grandchildren. I knew she spent a good deal of time on the computer with email, so I suggested that she put some of these stories onto the computer and send them to the entire family.

When she got home from the trip, she started sharing some of these stories and the response she got from the children and grandchildren was amazing. They were so interested, they began to collect stories and have since created a family history that continues to be written. Now her children are beginning to tell the grandchildren some of *their* stories. The closeness that results from this kind of sharing enriches the lives of everyone in the family!!!

It is my conviction that family ties are the most important and the most stabilizing relationships we will ever have. These are the relationships that can make our lives rich or can make them tragic. Everything depends on how we use and nurture them.

Over the years, however, social structures have changed dramatically. It used to be that families lived in the same physical proximity and neighborhoods provided social, spiritual, and psychological support. When I was a child, I lived in a neighborhood that consisted of all my grandparents, aunts, uncles, cousins and 500 families that made up the parish church community. We were actually brought up by the entire community. Let me share an example.

As children, we were told by our parents never to play in the street. One day, my brothers and a few friends took our wagon to the corner a block from our house. There the street took a 90 degree turn and became a steep hill for a half block. Thinking our parents could not see us, we were having fun riding the wagon down the center of the street and having a ball. However, my aunt, who lived at the bottom of the hill, could see us from her kitchen window and called my mother to let her know what was happening. When we got home, we were immediately punished and we learned very quickly that we could not get by with anything in the neighborhood because all the adults were all on the side of our parents!

Today, however, families often are separated by large distances in this country and even around the world. Extended family is spread out even more. But the fact remains: we need to be with other people if we are to be healthy and happy. For that reason, our relationships beyond family have become much more important, even essential to our well-being.

Napoleon Hill, in his book "Think and Grow Rich," spoke about the need for creating a circle of like-minded people (sometimes called a "support group") if we want to succeed at anything. Since that time, Marilyn Ferguson, in her book "The Aquarian Conspiracy," noted how small support groups have started to materialize all over the world. It seems that the human need for intimacy is mobilizing people at the unconscious level to fill that need. 12-Step programs proliferate for every kind of addiction; meditation groups, Curcillo groups, study groups based on "A Course in Miracles," small faith communities and many others make it clear that people feel a need to have a support community. Very simply put, we cannot live a full life without the love and support of others! Everywhere I teach, I suggest that my students create or join a support group if they are not already with one. Human support throughout our lives is a reality that none of us can live without!

The first support group that I joined lasted for more than 20 years, and I am still in touch with people from that group. Here in Indianapolis, we have such a group that meets once a week from 7 to 8 pm. We share the successes we have experienced in our lives, seek solutions to problems in our lives, share a group meditation and if time permits, look ahead to goals we would like to accomplish during the coming week.

I also belong to a priest support group that meets once a month, my Franciscan community with whom I meet weekly and a prayer community with whom I meet almost daily. I also connect with social networks on a regular basis, as well as with immediate family. All of these groups help me ground my life and my work!

Although families are scattered around the country and around the globe and old structures are no longer available, times are not the worse for these changes. What I see is the creation of a global family, where relationships cross over all the lines that used to separate us. What I see is an effort to build a truly universal mentality and a universal community!

Zalman Schachter-Shalomi and Ronald Miller are doing a wonderful work through their book "From Age-ing to Sage-ing." Having seen the separation of grandparents from grandchildren, they are going around the country helping older individuals understand their value as "mentors" because of their life experience. These authors suggest that all older people who have such valuable life experience take time, when they can, to share their insight with the younger generation. In carefully prepared workshops, they show participants how they can take advantage of opportunities that bring them into contact with younger people. This can be a time for sharing something from their past life that will help a young person better understand the life process or even to help a young person through a difficult life experience. These workshops also help participants to *create* situations where they can share with young people.

I had such an opportunity when I visited Uluru-Ayers Rock in the center of Australia. Every day I went to the same restaurant for all three meals. I was served by the same young people and took the opportunity to ask them about their lives, why they were working there, etc. I also shared a bit about my life, my work and my travels. It was interesting to note how these young people began to look for me at mealtime and how eager they were to continue our conversations. I felt that I was mentoring them the same way my grandmother mentored me when I was their age. All of us walked away from these encounters enriched with more understanding about life and filled with the joy of personal, loving and interesting human contacts.

During one of my sabbaticals I lived in Israel for four months. One day, while walking through the New City, I saw a notice for a folk dancing class to begin that week. Being a dancer since I was a very small child, I made a point to enroll in the class. I met some wonderful and interesting young people with whom I was able to share a great deal. My hope was that by giving them insight from my own personal experience, I could help them to enrich *their* lives and help them to look more creatively into their *own* future. But the learning was not just in one direction. I learned a great deal about the Jewish culture and life in Jerusalem. We had such great fun together those evenings. I fit in so well, I began to wonder if, in my German-Polish background, there were Jewish roots!

I think it is important to teach children from their earliest years about relating to everyone and to be aware of the *global* community. That kind of approach was not given to me as a child. Coming from a closed Roman Catholic community, we were forbidden to go into non-Catholic churches without permission of the pastor. I got the impression that Roman Catholics somehow were different and better than non-Catholics. So strong was this training in me that I hesitated to sit next to anyone on the bus or trolley not knowing if they were Roman Catholic or not.

Now, as the Founding Director of an inter-faith center, I am very aware that faith or gender, ethnic background or any other category is of no consequence. People are people the world over, and everyone has something unique and wonderful to offer society. In fact, our differences are the very things that enrich the lives of the global community,

When I was growing up, we had next-door neighbors who were from Poland. All the children married into other Polish families, except the youngest son, who fell in love with a lovely Italian woman. The neighborhood was all astir because they considered this a "mixed" marriage. At the wedding reception half of each dinner plate was covered with Polish food, the other half with Italian food (including pizza, which I had never tasted). I clearly remember the unique experience of that wedding and have been eating pizza ever since! Just recently, I saw this couple and they are happily married for over 50 years! Truly, our world has become a global village and it is expected that we are all getting "mixed up" into a wonderful international soup. What a fantastic idea!!!

As a child I had no idea that I would one day meet and befriend people from all over the world. Nor did I realize that people everywhere are essentially the same. They want to love and to be loved! At this point in my life, I have an "extended family" that continues to grow and continues to give me support no matter where I am on the planet. What a marvelous development for the 21st Century!

I do not intend to imply that human relationships on this earth are perfect or that they can be perfect. I do believe, however, that we are moving toward universal awareness that we are all one family – the human family. Like any family, we have challenges working and living with one another, but we are making progress. The very fact that we are aware of circumstances and events around the globe is helping to create an inclusive mind-set. Once that happens, it is only a matter of time until unity and acceptance become a reality.

Here are some suggestions for practical application of the above material:

1. Do you keep in touch with your family, either physically or by correspondence? Do you need to work on a relationship in your family?

2. If you are older, do you have (or can you create) opportunities to be with younger folks so that you can share some of your life experience with them? Get the book, "From Age-ing to Sage-ing" and find out how you can help young people by sharing

your life experience. -- If you are younger, do you have (or can you create) opportunities to be with older people and ask them about sharing some important events in their lives?

3. Do you know your neighbors? If not, can you make a point of getting to know one or the other of them? -- If you already know your neighbor(s), go out of your way for one of them so that they know you care.

4. Do you belong to a support group, a book club, a small faith community, a church group or any network that can support you in your ideals? If not, perhaps you might think about finding out what is available in your area and visit one or the other of these groups. Another option: start your own support group with people who think the way you do.

5. Take time to visit someone who is sick, whether they live at home or in a hospital. Drop a card in the mail to someone who is sick, just to let them know you are thinking of them.

5. *Our Relationship with the Spirit World*

By way of review, let me remind you that trying to communicate about the world of spirit is challenging! As we said earlier, it is impossible to adequately express anything in the spirit world. Spirit is one, has no parts, does not exist in time or space, (therefore has no up or down, no in or out.) and simply *is*. In this chapter, we will examine our relationship with God, with angels and finally with saints.

a. God

Words, because of their limit, make it challenging to talk in any meaningful way about the unlimited reality of spirit! The term "God," for example, points to the general and total reality of Spirit, a reality that is infinite. But we will never be able to fully comprehend what that means!

Using a comparison, the term "world" can point to the universe, which is another reality that we will never be able to fully comprehend. But "world" can also point to planet earth, which is a limited reality and one we have little difficulty understanding. Sometimes we use "world" and "universe" interchangeably and this usage can be confusing. In the same way, the word "God" can point to all spiritual reality but other words can be used also, for example, "Cosmic Energy", "Universal Intelligence", etc.

Therefore, from the outset, we have a challenge trying to talk, in any meaningful way about this unlimited reality! On the other hand, everyone can relate to the spiritual side of our humanity. For example, we all experience "mind", we experience "love," and are powerfully affected by "beauty." All of these experiences give us first hand "knowledge" of spiritual reality, which we can also identify as God.

Think back to a time when you were moved by a beautiful scene or object. In a moment like that, something in your life and person changes and you can never be the same again. - I recall when I was only about 14 years of age and I was looking at the Sunday newspaper on the living-room floor. I came upon a full-page ad for a Sadler Wells Ballet performance of "Coppelia" by Leo Delibes. I knew nothing about ballet and had never experienced a ballet, but for some reason, I knew I had to attend this performance.

When I asked my mother for permission to go, she suggested I find someone from the neighborhood who might want to go with me. I asked friends, classmates, and family members and the response I got from everyone was: "What's a ballet?!" In the end, I went to the performance alone. I will never forget the moment when the French horns began the overture and I heard a live orchestra for the first time in my life. As the ballet progressed, I found my self in a state I had not been in before. It was euphoric!

When the performance was over, I didn't want to move. I just wanted to be with the experience forever! I waited for the entire theatre to clear and then I went quietly onto the street where I walked, for what seemed like hours. During that time, I found myself talking to God. I connected with God in a way that changed my life!

Years later, when I was studying music at Case-Western University in Cleveland, OH, I came across a doctoral dissertation on "The Essential Similarity between Religious and Esthetic Experience." Only then, did I understand that coming in touch with "Beauty" in the ballet, was the same as coming in touch with God.

My point is, when we come in contact with an *experience* like this, we come in touch with God. Any personal contact with "Beauty" is contact with the world of Spirit and with God. The principle is this:, Relating to "Beauty" is relating to God.

Experiences of love give us the same kind of insight. I must have been in my late teens when I fell in love for the first time. I was floating on a cloud, feeling like I was going to explode with happiness and seeing life in a completely different and marvelous way! St. Paul said: "God is Love!" That means, when we are in touch with "Love" we are also in touch with God. Like experiences of Beauty, so, too, love experiences give us first-hand knowledge of God and insight into our connection with God.

As an educator, it is a challenge *trying* to help others understand a relationship with God. The examples given above are examples of an *emotional* connection with God. However, an *intellectual* experience can connect us to God also. For example, when I was a child, the nuns tried to help us relate to God by describing God as an old man sitting on a cloud with a big book, looking over the world and seeing everything. That kind of intellectual knowing got me to relate to God but through an experience of fear! I related to God all right, but like I related to a policeman! I kept thinking: "God is watching me all the time!" This kind of intellectual "knowing" creates a different kind of relationship with God!!!

Today when I am working with children, I know the image of the old man on the cloud is not an effective one for youngsters of the 21st Century. Instead, I use the image of "Energy." Children today know that energy is everywhere: in clothing, in the floor, in the earth, in air, in outer space, etc. When I ask them to think of God as Universal Energy, they get some idea of the Infinite. But at the same time, identifying Energy in them and around them can create a much more positive and intimate relationship with "God"!

However, I never give children an intellectual approach only. I always add a personal *experience* of God in meditation. I ask them to close their eyes, help them to relax their bodies, direct their attention inward and lead them into a guided meditation. At the end of the exercise, when they are very still and quiet and their eyes closed, I ask them to reflect on how they feel. Always, there is a profound silence and the students experience a "Peace" that gives them a wonderful experience! They actually "feel" their connection with God.

I do not what to imply that "intellectual knowing" cannot lead to a valuable relationship with God. It can!!! In fact, I believe many scientists are modern-day mystics! Deepak Chopra, author of "How to Know God," for example, began his career as a medical doctor and is now teaching spirituality. Bruce Lipton, author of "Biology of Belief," is also in the medical field but left a tenured position to build a bridge between biology and spirituality. As I read these authors, and others of like mind, I find myself overwhelmed by the beauty and power of "Nature" and experience the presence and peace of the Divine!

In much the same way, I sense my relationship with God when I view films like "What the Bleep Do We Know". At the end of this film, the experience was so powerful that I wanted to sit in the quiet, just to "be" with the great mystery that is Mother Nature!!!

Please note that all of these experiences make us aware of God's presence within us and when we are conscious of these experiences, our relationship with God grows and changes.

Buddha developed a life-transforming relationship with "God" (although in Buddhist theology they do not use that word). After living a protected life of pleasure, the Buddha encountered a sick man, a poor man, a beggar, and a corpse. In an effort to find some meaning in all these challenging life experiences, he left his wife and family to live a solitary, disciplined life. One day as he sat quietly under a pipal tree in meditation, "Truth" came to him. This relationship with the "Divine" changed his life forever! He spent the rest of his life teaching others that they too could find nirvana (heaven) – which is nothing more than a conscious awareness of union with the Divine. - Please note: the tool for developing this personal relationship with God was meditation.

The scientific community knows the importance of quiet for "touching" the reality we call "Infinite." Herbert Benson in his book, "The Relaxation Response," spoke about the power of this place of quiet. Being in a place of total relaxation and quiet can create an environment where the body can heal itself, lower blood pressure, and slow down the heart rate. The Simontons, in their book "Getting Well Again," showed how being in this quiet can assist cancer patients toward total remission and healing. Dr. Bernie Seigel in his book, "Love, Medicine, & Miracles," describes how meditation can affect healing of any disease. These authors, and many more, are showing how anyone can use God energy, to which we are all connected. Meditation is our becoming aware of God, who is present in us always!

Our lives are filled with the presence of the Divine, but a good deal of the time we don't pay attention. So often we allow these experiences to pass by and they get lost forever. Jesus said: "The Kingdom of God is here at hand, it is within you!" (Luke: 10:9 & 17:21) But he didn't teach with words only, he also taught by his example. Throughout his life, Jesus was constantly going into the quiet: before his public ministry he was alone in the desert for 40 days; during his busy active life, he frequently went to a garden at night, or to a mountain top, to be in the quiet. His teaching is quite specific: "When you pray, enter into your inner chamber, lock your door, and pray to your Father who is in secret, and your Father who sees in secret shall Himself reward you openly." (Matt: 6:6) He went on to say that those who understand how to be in a state of conscious awareness of the Divine, would see the same results as he, himself, was producing: "Whoever believes in me will do the works that I do and will do greater ones than these..." (John 14:12)

The saints and holy people of all religions connected with God in meditation and in that state directed this Energy in every direction. For example, they were able to read minds and hearts, see at a distance, heal people physically, mentally and spiritually etc.. But, like Jesus, they taught that everyone had the same potential. They taught that we are all connected to the same "Divine Energy" and anyone who developed his/her connection with God could produce the same results.

The question at this point is this: Are you developing your connection with God!!!???

b. Angels

We have said over and over again that in the spirit world there is only *one*. However, because we cannot even conceive anything as simply one (without parts), we have to use language that speaks of parts. For that reason, the idea of angels has been with us for millennia. I hope that the following discussion will help you understand a bit more about the idea of "angels" and how you can relate to it.

"Angelus" in Latin means, "a messenger." In theology, an "angel" is said to be the means or the channel through which God communicates to us and/or with us.

I think most people today think of "angel" as being a human figure with wings – only because so many artists have depicted angels in that way. These images, however, are only symbols that point to "Divine Communicator." For example, in the Old Testament, God told Abraham not to kill Isaac. Because artists cannot draw a spiritual entity, they have depicted the angel as a human being with wings, hovering in the air above Abraham, as if speaking to him. However, the picture is only symbolic. We really don't know what the experience of Abraham was. It just might have been that Abraham heard a voice in his mind (as we often do!). The important fact, however, is that God communicated a message and Abraham received it. In this case a "thought" in the mind of Abraham can be referred to as *"angelus"* because it is the means by which God communicated to Abraham.

Angels have also been symbolized as beings of light. At one of my Angel retreats, a woman shared a personal experience. Her husband died and she had asked for some kind of sign that he was happy and at peace. One night, she woke up to see three light forms at the foot of her bed. Although these light forms were not shaped like human beings, she knew for certain that the center form was her husband and the other two, his brothers (who had also died). She wasn't frightened at all; in fact she remembers a wonderful peace that came over her and an absolute assurance that her husband was happy and at peace. – Once again, this was a Divine message, one that came through images of light, which can also be called *"angelus"*.

But God does not have to be limited to images of humans, or of light, or inner voices. – God can communicate in a million different ways.

I remember a friend of mine sharing this story. Her father was ill and not expected to live. She had always had a difficult time communicating with him and there was some "unfinished business" she had to resolve with him before he died. Before going to bed one night, she asked for information that would help her find a way to reach her father and to resolve the differences they were experiencing. The next day, she planned to pick up her husband at the airport but when she arrived there, she was told that the plane was going to be about 4 hours late.

Because she was a full hour from home, she decided to go to a nearby shopping mall to kill some time. When she got there, she passed a movie theatre where a film was going to begin in just a few minutes. She decided to attend the movie and within the context of the story she found exactly how she could approach her father. She came out of the movie in tears, overcome with joy at having received this information. – In a real sense, the movie in this case was the messenger and therefore can be pointed to as *"angelus"*.

Perhaps you, the reader, have experiences of your own in which information you needed for your life came to you during a conversation with a friend, or from the pages of a book, or as a flash of insight. In these cases, the friend and/or the book can be referred to as *"angelus"* but the important reality is that God communicated the information through these media. The flash of insight, too, is simply God communicating to you through the medium of your own mind, in which case, the mind is *"angelus"*.

Please note the names of Angels in the Bible. Michael means "one who is like God." A person, therefore, whom we refer to as a "holy" person, for example, Mother Theresa, can certainly be called "Angel." - Gabriel means, "Soldier of God." Therefore, a person who "fights" for what is good, for example, Martin Luther King, Jr., can also be pointed to as an "Angel." - Raphael, "Healer of God" might refer to the water of Lourdes in France. In this case the water is the "Angel." In each of these cases, the holy person or the one fighting for justice or even the water in which healing happens can be referred to as "angel", the medium by which God communicates to us.

Perhaps the above explanation will help you to realize that angels are not a reality of the past or some special reality that happens to only a few or only in very special places. My hope is that you now understand that God is talking to you more frequently than you realize, and that you have angels around you, all the time!

Let me conclude this section on Angels with this poem:

ANGELS

In the Spirit
World we know,
There is only ONE:
Neither time nor space,
No parts or place,
No moon or stars or sun.

But as humans
We must deal
With a world of "parts":
Rings and things
And what one sings
Is where the Spirit starts.

God is one
And in us all
Always there to be
Friend and Guide,
Lover, too,
Helping us to see.

When we need
A helping hand,
God is always there.
If we ask
That's half the task
Some may call it prayer.

Mind Divine
Communicates
With us every day.

"Angelus"
Means messenger,
Such a simple way!

Light can be
An angel sign
Even in the mind,
Greeting cards
And telephone calls –
Cherubs of some kind!

People, books,
Songs and films
Can be angels, too!
Just as long
As they relay
God's messages to you!

Listen well
And you will hear
Eternal chimes of Love,
Ancient voices
Inner choices
God's Angelic glove

c. Saints

I want to remind you again that when speaking about the spirit world we are dealing with a serious communication difficulty. Because language is always inadequate, we have to face the challenge of constant paradox. As we said above, the spirit world is one, but already in this section we have made three divisions: God, Angels and now Saints. But if the spirit world is one, how can we have parts? The answer to that question is "I don't know!" So we will continue, in this chapter, making believe that what we say is somehow helping you understand your relationship with the spirit world – and in this section with the idea of saints.

Saints and holy people of all religions have always been important in organized religion. These are people who have developed the skills of mental prayer (meditation) and who had personal experiences with mystical phenomenon. They are, in fact, models for those of us who are interested in being more effective with the spiritual dimension of our own lives.

First of all, let me share a few insights about my understanding about saints. When I was a child, the Franciscan Sisters who taught in our grade school tried to help us understand that saints were special. I got the impression that they were "chosen" by God and that was the reason they were saints. In my own mind, I visualized God carrying a great big bucket of "grace" and then "He" went around the world, looking for someone on whom "He" could dump this "grace." Once you got "dumped on," you had no choice: you became a saint! I really liked that idea, because it got me "off the hook", so to speak. I didn't have to worry about becoming a saint because God had not dumped on me!

Now that I have grown up, both physically, intellectually and spiritually, I have come to see this whole situation in a completely different light. With the help of the scientific community and my own experience, I know now that the potential, which was present in the lives of the saints, is the same potential present in *every* human being!!! Every one of us can become a saint, if only we choose to develop the skill of meditation (mental prayer).

Let me use a couple of examples. St. John Vianney, the Cure' of Ars (1786-1859), was not very intelligent. In fact, he was considered to be average at most! I remember hearing the story of how he was finally allowed to be ordained a priest. The bishop had come to examine the student candidates, most of whom were extremely bright. After interviewing several of them, the Bishop believed that the entire class was exceptional so he decided to ask only one question of the rest of the candidates. When John Vianney went to the Bishop, he was asked a question which was one of only a few he could answer.

Later as a priest-confessor, St. John became so skilled in meditative prayer that he was able to read people's minds, give advice that came from a spiritual source (surely not from his own personal experience or background) and had unusual powers of healing.

Today, the scientific community is studying mystical phenomena such as "reading minds and hearts," "tapping into Universal Intelligence" and "healing." However, in science these phenomena are called "psychic." But whether you use the term "mystic" or "psychic", the human experience is the same.

As a teacher of meditation, I know that *any* human being who meditates regularly, can develop these skills. In other words, anyone can become a saint! It is not a matter of God "dumping" grace on anyone; it is a matter of a person making a choice to develop the skill of meditation.

Let me use another example. In Catholic circles most everyone knows that if you have lost anything, the saint you need to get in touch with is St. Anthony. Here is a story that I heard just today. LuLu lost a whole ring of keys that detached itself from a larger ring. She left Indianapolis to visit her mother in Cincinnati and when she arrived at her mother's home to open the gate, she realized that the ring of keys was gone. Immediately she turned her eyes upward and prayed: "Tony, Tony look around, something's lost and must be found." When she returned to Indianapolis she went to the restaurant where she intuitively knew she must have dropped them. However, after asking at the lost and found, she was told there were no keys. She continued to use the prayer and still later in the month, she returned to the same restaurant and asked again. To her delight, the keys had been found and returned!!!

Scientifically, the situation can be explained like this. The spirit world is *one* and LuLu's prayer can be described as tapping into Universal Intelligence. The image of St. Anthony is merely the cueing mechanism to contact Universal Intelligence. Once the contact has been made, LuLu "knows" that the keys are in or near the restaurant. The person who found the keys in the parking lot also gets a "message" from Universal Intelligence to take the keys into the restaurant and not into any of the other shops on the lot. LuLu's persistence in continuing to ask for the keys at the restaurant comes from Universal Intelligence.

Theologically, the situation can be explained like this. LuLu was able to find the keys, through the intercession of St. Anthony. The image of Anthony is the means by which LuLu is able to tap into God-Consciousness. The image of Anthony is only the cueing mechanism to contact God. God directs the person who found the keys, as well as LuLu who lost the keys.

Whether you use a scientific explanation or a theological one, the result is the same.

d. Visions

There are an unlimited number of psychic (or mystical) experiences that we could discuss but this field is much too vast to attempt to consider all of them! Therefore, I will conclude this section by spending a bit of time on the experience of mental images, sometimes referred to as visions.

Visions can be described as "seeing mentally." It is something that is common to everyone and something we do on a daily basis. For example, in the morning when you awaken and begin planning your day, you are actually mentally "seeing" what you will be doing in the future. You do the same thing when you are planning a vacation.

Unfortunately, I think most people define visions as images outside themselves and consider this phenomenon as something related to "chosen" individuals. These ideas couldn't be further from the truth!

Again we must go back to the basic principle that **it is impossible to adequately express anything in the spirit world.** Keeping this idea in mind, how can a person explain "seeing" something that no one else "sees"? Let me use an example. I heard about this situation some time ago. A mother was in one part of the country and her daughter was hundreds of miles away at college. The daughter was driving home in a terrible storm when she slid off the road and totaled the car. The mother was at home reading in the living room while her husband was watching TV. At the exact moment of the accident, the mother knew immediately that something serious had happened to their daughter.

Later that evening, when the daughter was safely in the hospital, she asked to call her parents. The mother was relieved to know that the daughter was going to be OK and then explained to her how she knew about the accident the minute it happened. -- Please note, the mother received the information from the inside, not from any outside source. This kind of experience can be called a "vision" or "seeing at a distance".

Seeing mentally can also explain famous cases of visions. Medjugorie is a little village in Croatia where several children were having daily visions of the Blessed Mother. However, the visions were not in any one place. For example, if one of the children traveled to another city, they continued to have the visions.

I had the opportunity of being with some of these children in Medjugorie when they were having a vision in the choir loft of the parish church. Their eyes were opened but they were not focused. They seemed to be staring at a blank wall and if anyone waved a hand in front of them, they would not be disturbed in the least. The images that they were experiencing existed in their minds.

In order to explain the process to the group of pilgrims with whom I was traveling, I decided to create a personal experience for each of them. I wanted to make it clear that the visions of the children were not attached to the place, Medjugorie. The experience of the children took place *inside* each child.

In order to make this point clear, I took the group to Apparition Hill (where the children had their first experience). There I had the group form a circle, hold hands and close their eyes. Then I led them though a guided meditation. I asked them to mentally "see" the Blessed Mother floating above the ground in the center of the circle. Then I asked them to have a "conversation" with Mary. This dialogue lasted only 5 minutes. When I brought them out of the meditation, most of these people had had a profound experience, some were in tears. For some, that meditation was the highlight of the trip. They began to realize that, just as the children can have a "vision" of Mary, so can all of us!

I believe that the message of Medjugorie is this: Just as the children can go into an altered state of consciousness (a meditative state) and "see" and "visit" with the Blessed Mother, so too, can anyone else go into meditation and have a similar experience.

Although theologically we describe these kinds of experiences as "visions," scientists refer to them as examples of "clairvoyance."

Mental "knowing" can also take the form of mental "hearing." Have you ever found yourself mentally trying to solve a problem in your life and carrying on a conversation with yourself? As you "see" the situation and "discuss" it mentally, you understand more and more until finally you come upon a solution! This kind of experience can be put under the heading of "vision" also, even though you may think of it as "audio" in nature. The scientific term for this kind of mental "audio knowing" is "clairaudience."

In my own life, I have had the experience of clairaudience over and over again. For example, when I tell myself at night that I want to get up at a particular time the next morning, I often have the experience of actually hearing my name being called out or I hear a knock on the door but there is no one to call my name or knock on the door. These experiences are not taking place in the external world, they are happening in my head.

Mental information can also come to us through our physical bodies and this kind of knowing is referred to as "clairsentience". When I am teaching the Silva Meditation Class I give the students an exercise that will prove they have the ability to "see" at a distance. Some of them receive the information through physical sensations in their own bodies. For example, one of my students was mentally examining an individual who was not physically present and as she got into the experience, she began to feel discomfort in her abdominal area. The fact was the person she was mentally "examining" had a stomach ulcer and the information was coming to her in her own physical body.

Another experience of clairsentience that is rather common can be described in a personal experience of my own. One day, I was invited to a party and was feeling excited and expectant about the evening. However, when I arrived and found myself standing in a small group, I began to feel very uncomfortable and embarrassed. As I looked around at the people near me, I noticed a younger person in the group who was very quiet and seemed rather nervous. I made a point of approaching him and struck up a conversation. I asked his name, where he came from, how he knew and met our host, etc.

As we continued the conversation, the feelings of discomfort and embarrassment left me. I then realized that initially I was feeling what this young man was feeling. As soon as he began to feel comfortable, all of my feelings changed and we both had a wonderful evening!!!

All of us have the potential of clairvoyance, clairaudience and clairsentience. Some have one or the other of these skills by nature but all can be developed by anyone. Every human being has the capacity of mentally receiving information through all of these avenues. Let me remind you that the saints and holy people of all major religions throughout the centuries exhibited these skills in one way or another. Recall the shepherds in Bethlehem who "saw" and "heard" angels. Joan of Arc who was directed by "voices." Martin Luther King, Jr. who had a "dream"! Lincoln who "saw" the United States as a free nation for all people. Pope John XXIII who "envisioned" a truly universal Church that would create a loving and compassionate world!   Ghandi who "saw" a free and independent India, etc., etc.

All of the above human experiences can be put under the general category of "visions" and are experiences that are common to every human being. My hope is that you will understand more clearly the potential *you* have, so *you* can use this potential to improve your own life and the lives of everyone in this universe!!!

Some suggestions for practical application

1. Pay attention as you drive to work to the beauty of the surroundings and reflect on how you feel!

2. Use a Hermitage morning or evening meditation and pay attention to the peace that comes in that experience.

3. During the day, pay attention to whom or to what is an angel in your life.

4. Smile at others, greet people, or be friendly in other ways and be an angel to others.

5. Give some thoughts to the people who have modeled for you in the past. They are your saints.

6. The place where you live and work is a holy place as long as you are putting God's presence there by your example!

7. Every morning, take time to "vision" the up-coming day and in the evening "look back" to what you have accomplished. Pay attention to how you "see" mentally.

8. When you are driving alone, turn off music or the radio and "be" in the quiet. Then pay attention to the conversation that goes on in your mind.

6. Conclusion

Spirituality is nothing more than the way you relate – to things, to plant and animal life, to human being, to the world of spirit, etc. In this chapter, we have suggested a more universal way in which you can relate to all of these dimension of our world. My hope is that you will not only see a broader "picture" of realitiy but that you will make a decision to move into a more universal way of relating yourself,

What happens to all of us on Planet Earth will depends on how we choose to relate to every dimension of the universe. If we want universal peace, we must think "Universal Peace!" If we want our environment to be beautiful, we must think "Universal Beauty." If we want to live in a world of love we must think "Universal Love." Our future depends on what you and I do with the power of our MIND.

Are you ready to make some changes in how you think about your relationship to things, plant and animal life, all human beings and to the world of Spirit?

VI

CREATING THE FUTURE

In our Franciscan approach to spirituality, practical application is very important. St. Francis was a down-to-earth person who was very involved in the practical experience of daily living. When I was being trained to give sermons or homilies, we were taught to think first of the practical application we wanted to achieve and then work back to the material that would create the foundation for that application. The question we were always asking was how does this help me and others live our lives with more meaning and more joy?!

In this final section of "Success: Full Thinking", I want to offer some ideas on how thinking can affect the future of our own personal lives as well as the lives of everyone on the planet and in the universe. Our minds are connected to an unlimited energy source. You can call that God, Universal Intelligence, Cosmic Energy or anything else. The fact is that we have the power to create a better world and we can do it if we so choose.

In this limited space, I can only deal with a few areas of life but once you get the idea of the applications, my hope is that you can apply this material to whatever area of life is important to you. I truly believe that if enough people understand the process, and a sufficient number of people get involved, we can create a world of opportunity for everyone, a world dominated by love and compassion, and a world where all human beings can live in peace.

1. Organized Religion

Because I am a Franciscan Friar, a priest in the Roman Catholic Church, and a person who has had a passion for spirituality all my life, this is the area where I am most competent and where I have the greatest insight.

a. Servant Leadership

To begin with, I think it important to make a clear distinction between organized religion and spirituality. I think the presumption, for some, is that these two areas are one and the same. In fact, they are two distinctly different areas. When my students ask me to explain the difference, I say, half jokingly and half seriously: "Religion is big business; spirituality is your connection with God."

Theoretically, organized religion *should* be dispensing spirituality, but I don't think that is necessarily true today. If you look at the person of Jesus, you will find that he had very little, if any, structure. He was involved almost totally in spirituality. That situation was true until 313 AD when Constantine began to impose Roman structures on organized religion. Before that, Christian communities met in small groups, which were very diverse. There were no institutions like "priesthood" as we know it today, nor institutions like "cardinal" or "pope." When the Christian community gathered to celebrate Eucharist, the group would determine who in the group would preside. Of course, that leadership might change at each gathering. Please note that in this kind of structure, the system is based on power rising out of the community upward.

All of this began to change, however, when Roman structures were imposed on the Christian community. Roman structures reversed the process so that power came from the top down. These are the systems that have developed over the past 1700 years and what we know today as "patriarchal" systems. What we have now is a top-heavy structure preoccupied with law, authority, politics, wealth and power. In my view, it is not balanced with spirituality.

The basic message of Jesus on love and compassion is getting pushed to the side.

Pope John XXIII was concerned about this situation and for that reason called the Second Vatican Council to begin a return to the ideal of the founder, Jesus Christ. This process of returning to the ideal of the founder was directed also to religious communities within the Church, including our Franciscan Order.

Significant changes in our Franciscan structures are taking place but not too many people outside of religious communities can see these changes. They certainly are not content for the front pages of our newspapers or cover stories on TV news!!! Let me tell you of the changes that have happened in our Franciscan Province.

When I joined the Order, patriarchal structures ruled supreme everywhere. Our Provincial and his staff told everyone in the province where to go and what to do. Subjects were never allowed to question superiors. Fear of punishment was the motivating power. There was a clear distinction between "the good" and "the bad," between "Catholic" and "non-Catholic," male and female, etc.

The Vatican Council put forward a completely different approach, which the friars immediately began to study. Those of us who were studying for the priesthood, used the Vatican Documents as a textbook. We had no choice but to know these documents inside and out! After being ordained to the priesthood, we had to continue studying the Documents because we were examined every year (for five years) by the theological faculty.

The Province created systems to educate all the friars, whether in studies or not. Little by little, we were schooled in the ideals of Vatican II, always thinking how the theory would show in our daily lives.

After several years, we produced a plan, which was launched at a weeklong conference. Every member of the Province had input in the planning of this meeting and no one was exempt from attending this meeting! With the help of professional facilitators, we made dramatic changes. We threw off the monastic structures, which Rome had imposed on us for hundreds of years. We determined what our priorities as a Province were to be. We planned our future. Then, at the end of the week, we elected our Provincial and his staff. We handed the results and directives of that week to our newly elected leadership and said, "This is your agenda."

Changes began immediately. Before Vatican II we lived in monasteries. Now we live in friaries where the atmosphere is more family oriented. In the past, most of our leaders were appointed; now they are elected, and when one's term of office is over, that person returns to the rank and file. In the past we were sent to a place and stayed there until our superiors told us to move elsewhere. Today leadership dialogues with each friar regarding placement in ministry, and friars can move from one ministry to another when they feel called to that kind of change.

At present, we no longer have a patriarchal structure with power coming from the top down. We have servant leadership, in which our superiors are considered servants and really do function in that capacity. For example, when I first entered the Order, the Provincial and his staff told everyone in the Province where they were to go and when. Now, if there is a request for help sent to the Provincial by a bishop, our Provincial will put a notice in the Provincial newsletter informing the friars of the position. If anyone feels called to do this kind of work, they can respond to the request. If no one responds to the request, the bishop is simply told that we don't have anyone to fill the position. Obedience truly is obedience to our conscience! When our Provincial comes for formal visitation each year, his question is always, "How can I help you in your ministry?"

Our structures now reflect much more clearly the kind of institution envisioned by St. Francis, structures that value the individuality of each friar and help us to create a brotherhood from the bottom up, as well as from the top down. Our Province has become a leader among the provinces in the USA and now we are creating inter-provincial meetings so that we can share our success, and help other provinces create similar and even better structures of servant leadership.

There is a real challenge today for organized religion to envision and implement structures like these. Religious Orders in the Catholic Church, especially women's communities, have restructured their systems and will certainly be a catalyst for further change in other departments of Catholic systems.

Perhaps the leadership of religious in the Church will help change diocesan structures. For example, in the average diocese, anywhere in the world, leadership almost always comes from outside the diocese. (In our Franciscan structures, leadership always comes from within our own constituency). In a diocese, the Bishop can only go up. (In our Franciscan structures, when a person completes his term of office, he goes back to the rank and file). In a diocese, the priests and religious may have little or no voice in the direction and policy of the diocese. (In the Order, our priests and brothers all have active voice in the direction and policy of the Province).

Radical change in the structure of our Order has taken more than 30 years to create but it has been done and it will be an ongoing process! If we can get people in other areas of organized religion to "see" the kind of structures that were in the minds of their founders, and get back to the basic ideals of love and compassion, community and servant leadership, I believe that massive change can happen. Only then will we be able to put spirituality back into its rightful place in organized religion. But please note, we must first create the reality in our mind's eye before anything can happen in the external world!!!!

b. Small Faith Communities

Years ago in Central and South America, numbers of ministers and priests of organized religion began to diminish dramatically either because vocations were few in number or because governments would not allow ministers and priests to function openly. In response to these changes, the people began to form small faith communities. These communities resembled the Church as it existed in the first 300 years after Jesus. The structure of each group is based on the personal talent and skill of the individuals involved and/or the need of those who are in the group. For example, those in the community who can read, proclaim the Scripture. Those who feel called to serve, carry Eucharist to the sick and elderly. Those who can sing or play musical instruments, lead the community in song, etc.

At present, especially in Central and South America, the entire Church is being restructured into faith building communities, which are, in many ways, more effective than traditional patriarchal structures. The advantages of these small groups are many: more people get actively involved; individual talents can be used for the good of all; there is no need for expensive buildings and maintenance; everyone knows everyone else; it is easy to set up a support system; spirituality (not dogma) is primary, etc.

The small faith community phenomenon has since been brought to the US and now is a significant movement seeking to build such communities within traditional parishes. Although very large parish communities still exist, small faith communities have become a sub-structure within the larger community. In these smaller units, members get to know one another better; they can support one another in their ideals; they can offer personal service to the needy; they can create meaningful community prayer; etc. In these small groups, *spirituality* is of major importance and Christian living is a top priority!

Some years ago, our Province brought a woman from South American to one of our Provincial Meetings where hundreds of our friars had gathered. She told the story of how her community got started with only five or six people. However, when the group began to grow, civil authorities forbade public assemblies and she and her young daughter were arrested. After torture and imprisonment, both escaped and eventually joined a small community in another country. Her faith was strengthened by this community, especially when there was suffering and persecution. Eventually she came to the United States.

When she had completed her story, one of the friars asked if we could help by sending priests into some of these areas. Without hesitation, she said: "NO, NO. We don't want priests!!!" The reason for this response was that everyone found the small faith communities more life giving than the traditional structure headed by a priest!

Let me add a few words here about 12-Step programs. The first of these was AA. The founders decided at the outset that the movement would not acquire real estate. The movement spread across the country and eventually around the world. Later it became a model for people with other addictions. Now there are 12-Step programs for people addicted to sex, gambling, over-eating, etc. Many people use the support group as a small faith community because they get their spiritual support there.

Graduates of the Hermitage programs all over the world have created similar groups that are called "Energy Circles." They, too, are support groups grounded in spirituality and offer the kind of support that some cannot get in traditional structures of organized religion. In these group meetings, the participants begin with a few minutes of silence so they can review the previous week and focus on success stories. After that, the group shares success stories, goals they might have accomplished, obstacles they have overcome, relationships that have healed, etc. At the end of the one-hour meeting, someone leads the group in a guided meditation. One of the first of these groups was started in the Cleveland area and continued for 20 years. When I moved to Indianapolis, we began another Energy Circle, which also continued for 20 years.

Support groups of any kind can serve as spiritual support. At present I have a support group in my Franciscan Community with whom I meet weekly. I also belong to a priests support group, which meets monthly. I also belong to a few social networks, which meets weekly or monthly. These groups are essential for supporting my spiritual, psychological, and ethical ideals!!!

We are all social beings and without human support we cannot remain stable. But our relationships must be built on high ideals and ethical standards. If you cannot be fed spiritually in traditional religious structures, perhaps you need to look for or create a community that can give you that kind of support.

An interesting phenomenon in all of the above is that so many of these small faith communities cross over the lines of organized religion. Do you suppose that spirituality is uniting people in a completely different way? If spirituality unites, perhaps we will have to rethink the categories we have created in organized religion (which have certainly done its share to divide!). -- You may find some of the ideas presented here, jarring your comfortable thought process and moving you to a thought process that is not so comfortable. If that is the case, then this book is doing its job!

c. Thinking "Outside the Box"

The purpose of this chapter is to help you to think creatively! Your mind is virtually unlimited! Creative thinking is the way that you can tap into a limitless reservoir.

When I was teaching in Australia, I met a truly outstanding member of the Secular Franciscan Order. His name is Dick Scallon. He told me the story of the parish community in Kalgoorlie, Australia. All Hallows Church is a community of several hundred families. At one point the Parish Finance Committee was advised that the parish could not rely on Planned Giving Contributions to fund the parish, its educational structure and its outreach programs. A few businessmen of the parish got together for a brainstorming session. They wanted to discover a service that was needed by the community, something they might be able to provide and at the same time generate income. They finally settled on a system of recycling, something that was needed by the community and something that would promote the health of Mother Earth.

They began St. Mary's Recycling, Inc., which, today, is a thriving business. It not only supports the Church and its ministries but is also helping the community dispose of its trash and eliminate a toxic landfill. The company developed another outreach to inmates from the local prison who, when released, were looking for jobs. Even while in prison, the prisoners train to operate machinery for St. Mary's Recycling so they can move into a job as soon as their detention period is completed. In order to show their appreciation for helping offenders, prison authorities allowed inmates to remodel pews from the 90-year old church so that they could be recycled into a new church. Handicapped individuals, also, were able to find work at St. Mary's Recycling.

This little parish community with this one creative idea has gotten into the headlines of the local papers and has caused Civic and State Governments to take notice. To date, St. Mary's Recycling, Inc. has received over $2 million in grants from Authorities for plant improvements, expansion, and equipment. This latest development is especially important in an isolated community where jobs are few and far between.

Please note, that even though this was a Roman Catholic Parish Community project, it was conceived with the entire city in mind! This is what I refer to as "thinking outside the box" and expanding thought process to include the entire planet. Imagine what organized religion could do if every church on the planet had this kind of creative thought process!!!

I might use our Center itself as another example. When I first began my preaching and teaching ministry in Indianapolis, I was working at a traditional Roman Catholic Retreat House on the north side of the city. The friars had welcomed me with open arms because I had packaged my programs using scientific terminology rather than theological terminology. As a result, when doing promotion and publicity for these programs we always contacted the local newspapers, radio, TV, community bulletin boards, etc. Of course, our clientele was a cross section of the local population, different ages, races, religions, etc.

After a few years, there were changes in the personnel at the Center and the programs that I was teaching were getting very large. Eventually, the Center came to be identified with our programs rather than with the Roman Catholic programs produced by the Retreat House. At that point, some of the friars were upset because they saw us losing our "Roman Catholic" image. It was for that reason that the Provincial Leadership eventually asked me to begin the Hermitage as an inter-faith Center.

The Franciscan Hermitage, Inc. was set up as a tax-exempt, not-for-profit entity attached neither to the Franciscan Order nor to the Roman Catholic Church. As a result, we were able to experience freedom that we could not have under either the Order or the Church. Because we were interested in working with the general public, with no consideration of church affiliation, we were able to work out of hotels, theatres, convention centers, etc., as well as churches of any denomination.

Today, the Hermitage has an international outreach only because of the structural changes we put into place disregarding the "divisions" of organized religion. Spirituality is a universal phenomenon and can be dealt with very successfully in a universal arena! But in order to do that, we had to think "outside of the box!"

I would like to add just one more idea to close this section. There are many writers today who are helping us to think "outside of the box." One is the Episcopal Bishop John Shelby Spong.

His books "Why Christianity Must Change or Die" and "A New Christianity for a New World" have helped me rethink many basic ideas regarding traditional Christianity. His challenge is not to destroy or give up faith; his challenge is to think about faith in a different way! Isn't that what Jesus did in his time???

Matthew Fox is another important author who can help us stretch and exercise our creative minds in the area of faith and spirituality. His early books, "On Becoming a Musical Mystical Bear" and "Whee, Wee, We All the Way Home," caught my attention and helped shape my creative thinking process. I can also recommend his volumes, "Creation Sprituality" and "Creativity". Not too long ago, I traveled to Louisville to experience what Matt Fox calls "Cosmic Mass." He has worked with young people, taught them the elements of good liturgy and then let them free to create. What they have produced is something that speaks in a meaningful way to young people and helps older individuals stretch their understanding and application of theological truth.

In my estimation, authors like these are shaping a meaningful future for organized religion but it will be some time before any of their ideas are commonplace. However, I do believe, as Pierre Teilhard de Chardin once said, that for any reality to happen, all that is needed is one person having a thought and a sufficient amount of time for that thought to materialize. I believe that as we think about the ideas contained in this book, we are helping to create a wonderful future that will bring peace and unity to our entire planet!!! One of our greatest assets is our mind, the place where we touch God and where together with God we can create all that is good, all that is true and all that is beautiful!!!

2. Science and Healing

Before we begin this section, let me review a few ideas. If you recall, we are saying time and time again, it is impossible to adequately express anything in the spirit world. This principle must also be applied to science.

The world in which we live is so extensive and complex that we will never understand its full reality. The universe is infinite but as limited human beings, we simply cannot comprehend that idea. Even scientists ask: How can we possibly discuss the universe in any definitive way? The answer to that question is simple: We can't. The only thing that scientists can do is create *theories* on how the universe works – but *no theory is complete*. In fact, you can count on theory updates on a regular basis, as long as human beings continue to study the universe.

What is important in this section of the book is that you reflect on this reality: the scientific theory you believe, will shape the world in which you live, will determine your life experience, and will control the decisions you make. All of us, whether we are conscious of it or not, subscribe to some scientific theory and live by that theory. Our belief about the world of science affects everything we do, every day!

For example, if you believe in the Theory of Newton – for every action, there is an equal and opposite reaction - this belief will affect the way you function. Suppose you have a headache. The theory is that pain in the head can be removed by taking an aspirin or some other medication. You take the medication, the pain leaves and you are satisfied. In this case, the body is treated as a machine, and the medication is used to "fix" the machine.

On the other hand, suppose you hold to the Quantum Theory, which holds that the body is a complex unit of energy fields and every part of the body is connected to every other part. If you experience a headache and believe in the Quantum Theory, you analyze that the headache is caused by blood vessels constricting because of stress. As a result, you go through a relaxation exercise, the stress disappears, the blood vessels no longer constrict and the headache disappears.

These differences in scientific thought process can make the difference between life and death. Suppose you believe "the doctor is the expert and I must do whatever the doctor says." Your doctor holds to Newtonian physics, considers the body as (s)he would any other machine and prescribes medication to "fix" the machine. This school of thought holds that the laws of biology and chemistry are immutable and so the doctor can predict what will happen based on his/her knowledge of biology and chemistry.

David had AIDS, went to the doctor and was told that he must take a regimen of drugs and if they do not work, he can expect to die (sometimes the doctor can give an estimated time of death).

George Melton, on the other hand, in his book "Beyond AIDS" describes what happened when he was told that he had AIDS. A client of his instructed him in the power of meditation, which he immediately began to study. His thought process led him to think "outside the box": "I know the laws of biology and chemistry, but if I go outside the box and apply meditation, perhaps I can use the laws of biology and chemistry in a different way." He began daily meditation, which stimulated his immune system. Now the laws of biology and chemistry began to operate in the direction of strengthening his immune system and eventually the disease disappeared.

David applied the traditional approach to medical science (following the doctor's orders), but George applied an alternative approach to medical science (applying meditation). The results for both were different because they each applied a different scientific theory.

This same scenario can be applied to cancer, as validated by O. Carl and Stephanie Simonton (radiologist and psychotherapist, respectively) in their book "Getting Well Again". Bernie Siegel, MD (in his book "Love, Medicine, and Miracles") described how meditation could be applied, with positive results, to any disease.

Psycho-neuro-immunology is a comparatively new science that has proven the direct effect of thought process on the immune system. The research is not only interesting but conclusive. Subjects allowed researchers to take blood samples to determine T-cell counts (this is a measure of the effectiveness of the immune system). Subjects were then put into a viewing room where they were shown negative images: pictures of the death camps during World War II, starving children in Africa, battered wives, etc. After 30 minutes, blood samples were taken again. These samples showed a significant *decrease* in the T-cell count.

The subjects were then put back into the viewing room and shown only positive and beautiful images: country and mountain landscapes, lovers walking down a lane, a mother nursing her child, etc. Again, after 30 minutes, blood samples were taken. This time the blood samples showed a significant *increase* in the T-cell count. The conclusion is clear: negative thoughts shut down the immune system; positive thoughts turn on the immune system!

With this insight, the rules governing biology and chemistry hold only if there is no outside influence. However, when the energy of human thought is applied to biology and chemistry an expanded system emerges with totally different results! In situations like these, science has to create a new theory to include a broader perspective than it had before.

Newtonian physics simply does not work when energy becomes part of the equation. But mind is only *one* energy field that can change physical reality. There are other sources that can produce and use energy in new and effective ways.

One of these is the Rife machine. R. Rife was born in 1888 and died in 1971. He was a brilliant scientist and inventor who designed and built medical instruments for Zeiss Optics, the US Government, and several private benefactors. In the summer of 1934, Rife used a super microscope to determine the frequency of a cancer-linked microbe. With a bio-energy machine that could reproduce that specific frequency at increased intensities, Rife was able to destroy the microbe in terminal cancer patients. He cured 16 out of 16 patients in La Jolla, CA. That machine today is called the Energy Wellness Instrument, which produces micro-current generated radio sound waves.

Unfortunately, this simple and non-evasive approach to cancer cure was a great threat to the established medical community. Before the American public could be alerted to this important discovery, and before controlled experiments could be done, the leaders in the traditional medical community put pressure on doctors who were using it and the technology went underground. In the 1980's and 1990's, when interest in "subtle energies" came to the fore, Rife's invention surfaced again and is now available for private use.

Dr. Alex Kinbaum is a retired MD who has become well versed in alternative methods of healing. He used the Rife machine for only a few days and was able to get off all his diabetic medication. - He also related this story to me. One day he was walking out of his home when a wasp stung him on the webbing between his first two fingers. The pain was extraordinary. He went back into the house, got onto his Energy Wellness Instrument and in only a minute or two, the pain completely disappeared, and there was no swelling!! At present, he is using it to improve his eyesight and tendonitis.

Even more dramatic is the following testimony. Mary is a high-school student whose father is a medical doctor. One day while at soccer practice, she fell and broke her ankle in three places. Her father was called in immediately and he decided that he would do the surgery himself. He wanted to make sure that his daughter had the best treatment available. He had to set bones and put in two pins. As soon as the surgery was over, he told the nurses that the Rife Energy Wellness Instrument was to be attached to the ankle and kept there 24 hours a day.

After one week, he ordered X-rays and both he and the X-ray technician were amazed. The bones had completely healed, in one week's time! – Because of the doctor's background, he would not allow his daughter to go without a cast, simply because it was hard for him to believe that the healing was complete. Therefore, he put on a cast, just to be sure, but removed it only a few weeks later because the healing was, in fact, complete. This doctor now thinks in a completely different way about his medical practice and has healing options that were unavailable to him before his daughter's accident!

Recently, a friend called to tell me his mother was taken to the hospital with a bowel obstruction. The doctor told him that if they cannot clear the bowel with chemicals, they might have to operate. Immediately I was thinking of the Rife Energy Wellness Instrument (See References for Wellness Pro®). If the mother could get on this instrument, dial up the frequency for the obstruction and apply the frequency at a sufficient intensity, the obstruction would disintegrate into a fine powder and pass out of the body easily, without the invasion of surgery!

We cannot go into all the alternatives in health-science technology; the field is far too large. However, I want to mention just a few items. There are more and more medical doctors who are moving into alternative methodologies in their practices, based, of course, on new findings in science. However, you are more likely to find new and alternative technologies more easily in the fields of dentistry and chiropractic. I have a brother and a nephew in each of these fields and with their help am schooled in approaches like homeopathy, nutrition, network spinal analysis, food supplements, electro–acupressure, etc,

I want to state again: the way you think about science and its application in your every day life will make a difference! If you think with an open mind about new technologies, they can become available to you. If you close your mind to these alternatives, you will close off wonderful and valuable life opportunities.

I find it difficult to understand the thought process of some health professionals. I once mentioned to a physician something about an alternative healing approach and without hesitation, he dismissed it, not knowing anything about it. This particular approach was outside his background of learning and, in his mind, not worth any consideration. I couldn't help recalling at that time a quote I found in a book on pyramid power: "Condemnation without investigation is the height of stupidity." In my mind, an educated person is one who knows (s)he doesn't know!!! If we are truly educated, we will be open to every kind of development and never make a judgment until there has been a thorough investigation.

Think how wonderful it would be if traditional *and* alternative health practitioners would get together to apply all their knowledge to effective healing. We need to think, "working together!"

3. Business

Business and economic systems on our planet are creating a greater space between the poor and the rich. The thought process behind this situation goes something like this: "I can do what I want in order to make as much money as I want!" Economic systems that immerge from this kind of thought process can create excessive greed in which little or no thought is given to the poor and disadvantaged. In fact, the focus becomes so centered on "the bottom line" that even employees become "tools" for improving "the bottom line." These systems can create serious injustice and endanger countless lives.

I believe we need to look at systems that will be satisfying and productive for *everyone* involved as well as safe for the environment and the health of Mother Earth.

a. Servant Leadership

One of the companies fostering a healthy thought process for business is the Greenleaf Center for Servant-Leadership. Robert Greenleaf wrote an essay in 1970 titled "The Servant as Leader" in which he says that true leadership

> " . . . Begins with the natural feeling that one wants to serve, to serve first. Then conscious choice brings one to aspire to lead. The best test is, do those served grow as persons; do they, while being served, become healthier, wiser, freer, more autonomous, more likely themselves to become servants? And, what is the effect on the least privileged in society? Will they benefit?"

Today, traditional forms of leadership are becoming outdated and new styles are emerging. In these new approaches, teamwork and community are important; leaders involve others in decision making; ethics and compassion are important; everyone involved in the company works toward continuing personal growth and development; all of which leads to improving the quality of the institution itself.

When we began the Hermitage in 1984, we were only five people but we wanted to apply the principles of servant leadership. All of us worked together to create our Statement of Purpose and to set goals. This task alone was time consuming but it was the result of a team effort. As a result, everyone took ownership of our goals; everyone developed a personal interest in the Center; and each member of the staff had a commitment to the tasks assigned to him/her.

Although several religious denominations were represented by our staff, we began each day with prayer (and/or meditation). Each member of the team took responsibility for preparing this prayer session one day a week. We also gathered at noon time for prayer before we had lunch. – In our meditation classes, we suggest to our students that they meditate at least once or twice a day so we felt we had to practice what we preach!

One day a month, we took off a full day for "retreat." We used this time to look back at what we had accomplished over the past month and forward to goals we wanted to achieve during the coming month. Sometimes, when there were personal difficulties among the team members, we used this day for group therapy. We would call in a professional to facilitate our communication and help us work through personal and relational challenges. For almost one year we used these monthly days of retreat to systematically read through and study a book on the consensus model. This theory teaches how decisions can be made with unanimous consent. It was a time consuming process, but it helped everyone to understand what the ideal was, and what the goals were. As an institution dedicated to personal growth and development, we felt we had to model what we were teaching if we were to be authentic.

Our time together as a team, however, was not all work. Sometimes our monthly days of retreat were overnights at a park or retreat center where we could go swimming together and have fun.

All of the above was part of a plan to create a team, a community. We did become emotionally close to one another as we worked together to build the Center.

These ideas on servant leadership are being taught by many valued educators today. Some of these are Stephen Covey, M. Scott Peck, Margaret Wheatley, Warren Bennis and many others.

Here are some characteristics of a leader who is servant:

i. Listening

Traditional leaders are known for their ability to communicate well and to make decisions. A servant-leader complements these skills with the ability to listen well. The idea is *to know the will of the group* being served.

I was attending an ecumenical service on the campus of a very prestigious theological school. The service had been planned for months. As the bishop was leaving his office to preside at the service, he told his secretary to phone ahead and tell the people in charge, that only ordained ministers were to be in the sanctuary.

The fact was that for months, non-ordained persons had already been assigned for this service and at the last moment, they were told that they could not participate. The individuals involved were insulted and angered, especially the women. After the service, when the entire community found out what had happened there was an uproar.

The Director of the School of Theology called the faculty, students and any others who were involved, to a meeting the following day and for one hour, the Director listened to the entire community. It was the community who drafted a letter to the bishop, stating their concerns, voicing their anger, exposing their embarrassment and requesting an apology. The Director was only the "secretary" who prepared the letter and sent it to the bishop.

I was amazed at the respect this meeting generated for the Director and for the school who honored the voice of the community in such a loving way.

You will know if a person is listening well, if you hear phrases like: "If I heard you correctly, you said..." or "Are you saying that...", or "How does that make you feel?" Listening is an important skill and one that is essential to a servant-leader.

ii. Empathy

In the example, above, the Director felt the anger and insult that the community was experiencing; he knew from his own experience what was going on inside each member of the community. There was no judgment on his part, no need to find excuses for the behavior of the bishop, nor to belittle the feelings of the community.

At this writing, the present mayor of New York makes it a point to ride the subway to work, instead of being driven to his office at City Hall in a limousine. By being with the citizens of the city in this daily routine, he knows, first hand, what his constituents are experiencing and has an opportunity to meet them personally. I understand, also, that this same mayor takes only $1 a year for his salary and gives the rest to the city. This is a person who is a servant-leader, one who knows how to feel what his constituents feel.

iii. Healing

Every organization is made up of individuals who have to live and work in close proximity. It is natural that challenging situations between individuals arise but the servant-leader is always there to heal relationships and generate love.

I was working in a school where the principal understood the importance of healing relationships. On one occasion, I knew parents who went into his office to complain about one of the teachers. As soon as he realized what the situation was, he told the parents that if they had any complaints about a particular staff member, he would have to call in that staff member so that he could hear both sides of the story. If the parents refused to speak in the presence of the staff member, the principal refused to listen to the complaint. But if there was a dialogue between the parents and the staff members, it was always resolved to everyone's satisfaction and the institution continued to thrive.

iv. Persuasion

In traditional leadership roles, authority often sends directives downward with the expectation that rules and regulations will be followed. A servant-leader uses another approach. By explaining the details of a particular situation, offering alternative solutions and even getting input from the constituency, the servant-leader persuades everyone involved to see the logic of the solution being offered. In this way, individuals choose to follow the rules and regulations because they see that they are good for themselves as well as for the institution.

I had been asked to give a series of staff workshops at a school in which there were a great many challenges: the staff was stressed, the school was in a major transition from an all-girls' school to a co-ed institution and most of the staff had little experience with boys, many of whom were disruptive. It was toward the end of the school year and the staff was tired and emotionally stretched.

We met once a week, for one hour after school, for eight weeks. Basically the material had to do with personal growth and development, how we make choices, how to set goals, develop positive attitudes, etc. Just getting the staff moving in a positive direction in their personal lives helped them to change their attitudes and they were better able to cope with the stress.

By the end of the year, the school decided to enlist my help in creating structures for the following school year. Over the summer we constructed a system that demanded much more communication. The principal was to meet with the administrative team once a week *but* each member of the team was to meet with the principal either formally or informally each week. Each member of the team was assigned to work with five or six other members of the staff to form sub-teams that also met once a week. Each faculty member in turn created still other sub-teams with five or six students that also met once a week.

With this system in place, communication was facilitated from the top down, as well as from the bottom up. If the team at the top wanted to implement any changes, it sent an explanation of the situation into the entire network requesting feedback, suggestions, etc. from the bottom up. With this kind of involvement by everyone, most of the disciplinary problems disappeared in a short time, the atmosphere in the school was more positive, the stress was lowered, and the school began to thrive in a completely different direction.

In this system, nothing was demanded or commanded from the top down. The entire school was involved in "healing" the problems. The healing was not created by the leadership, it was facilitated by all and everyone was able to take ownership and credit for the results.

These are only a few characteristics of servant leadership but they will give you some idea how traditional patriarchal models of leadership differ from the servant-leadership model. It may interest you to know that companies like Starbucks, Southwest Airlines, Men's Warehouse, and other large companies are using the ideas of the Greenleaf Servant Leadership Center. I believe that more and more major businesses around the globe are becoming aware of the importance of people-based and ethic-valued structures. As more and more CEOs begin to think this way, our world of business and commerce will change for the better. When thought process changes for the better, it is only a matter of time before our world changes for the better!!!

b. Ethics

At the end of the 20th and the beginning of the 21st Centuries, several major scandals surfaced in the business world. Not only did executives take monies illegally but they caused many innocent people to lose their jobs and many more to lose some, if not all, of their retirement. The patriarchal model in business has produced a thought process that "more is better" and "I deserve more." Greed blinds those who are selfish and who seek to hoard money and material things. Often times, these "leaders" have no consideration for others, least of all the poor and/or the disadvantaged. The root of the problem lies in a lack of moral thought process!

This situation has created a major interest in the field of ethics throughout the business community. In the recently published volume, "The Heart of a Business Ethic," William Pollard wrote:

> "We need nothing less than a radical reformation of thought and action to include a renewed focus on the development of the character and integrity of the business leader, determination of a source for moral authority and a standard of right behavior that cannot be waived or modified."

Please note, the very first concern is for a "radical reformation of thought!" Only when the thought process changes can we expect to see a change in the external world.

Please note also, that when ethics is applied, the results are always positive for everyone involved. This kind of ethical change is already happening, but the media does not give coverage to this kind of change the way it does to the scandals mentioned above. However, let me share a few examples.

In his book, "Self-made in America," John McCormack begins his discussion of success by concentrating on personal growth and development. His philosophy is that you must be grounded yourself before you can ground a business. If you know how to set goals in your personal life and balance all the areas of daily living, it is an easy task to transfer these skills to a business.

When he was down and out, living on a beach, John met an immigrant businessman who became his mentor. When he learned what he could from this immigrant, he was told to find two other immigrants who started with nothing and who became successful by using their creative intelligence and by turning difficulties into opportunities.

John did find these people and learned well!!! Now, he and his wife, Maryanne, have a thriving business, called Visible Changes. It consists of a chain of beauty salons, which enrich their lives, the lives of their family, as well as the lives of the people who work the business and the customers who use the business. It is truly a people centered organization!!!

A priest friend of mine was invited to the 25th Anniversary celebration of Visible Changes and shared some details with me. The event was held at the Convention Center in downtown Houston for 1,500 people, not only the employees but also their families. It was a formal black-tie affair that lasted from late morning until 8 pm. Awards were announced and presented at a magnificent banquet that began at 6 p.m.

One of the woman beauticians had generated sales of $225,000 in one year and received a bonus that night of $29,000. Luxury sport cars were awarded for one-month use by employees who excel in management, hair styling, color, etc. In other words, everyone can succeed financially in the business, even those who are new to the company.

However, there is a wonderful balance in this company. John and Maryanne continue to visit each of the 17 salons on a regular basis and know all of their employees personally. Twice a year, they sit down one-on-one with every person in the company.

"During these talks, we listen, we learn, and we share our goals and dreams with our people. We also review the staff member's performance over the last six months and set performance goals for the future. We also give out bonuses and super-bonuses, and one of the great pleasures of my life is to hand out large rewards for superior work," John said.

They also have quarterly meetings in which they deal not only with business matters but help their employees to understand personal responsibilities like quality time with their children, keeping themselves healthy, etc. Unique to any business I know, at these quarterly meetings, John and Maryanne ask their employees to vote by blind ballot, on whether they want John and Maryanne to continue running the business. They let the employees know what their own sales are and what their salaries are. (John and Maryanne want their employees to be accountable but they have created this system to make themselves accountable to the employees.)

What is even more incredible is the fact the John and Maryanne have created their own school. It is spacious and beautiful, a place where the students want to be. However, the curriculum is not only professional; cutting hair, doing perms, applying makeup, etc.; half of it is dedicated to life skills: balancing a checkbook, getting a loan, using a computer, increasing self-esteem, etc. Visible Changes, at its own expense, is giving the young people who come to them, the education they were unable to get in public schools.

In my estimation, Visible Changes, and many other companies like them, are leading the American business world to a new ethic that can bring prosperity to everyone!!! These types of companies focus on high values, both human and economic! They are companies dedicated to the service of *everyone*, even the communities in which their shops are located. They are models that, hopefully, will guide and motivate young entrepreneurs in the future!!!

In preparation for writing this section of the book, I interviewed others who had smaller businesses but who were on the same ethical wavelength. Jerry Trupiano, for example, began an Operator Specialty Co. by the name of Osco. He is not only a good business man, but like John and Maryanne, a quality person with high moral and ethical values. He is a people person who built a people business.

He, too, had a team concept that included his customers, his vendors and his staff, all of whom were personal friends. His concerns were not for the business only, but also for the people in the company, the customers who used the company and those who supplied the company. Improving the quality of life for all these people was an essential part of the business. When staff gatherings were in order, for example picnics or Christmas Parties, they always included the spouses and children. He even created a lending department within the company so that staff could get interest-free loans for emergencies or special needs.

When I completed my interview with Jerry, I was very aware that he considered his work a ministry, in the same way that my work as a Franciscan and a Priest is a ministry.

When I am working with companies who use Servant-Leadership principles I pay close attention. It is a joy, for example, to walk into a Starbucks Coffee shop and carry on a friendly conversation, however brief, with people who are kind and gracious, who enjoy serving people, and who function as professionals. This is true also of people in ServiceMaster, another company that uses Servant-Leadership principles.

We could continue with this section of the book discussing creative thinking regarding, education, government, media, entertainment, ecology and every other area of 21st Century living but that would be impossible. We would need whole libraries, not just one book for each of these areas!!! Suffice it to say that no challenge is too large, no obstacle too dense, no problem too complex! Creative intelligence is unlimited and resides within each of us. As we learn to access this unlimited reservoir, we will be able to clarify our direction and resolve any problems whether that be from the past, in the present or in the future!   You are one with Universal Intelligence; *use it daily*!!!

4. *Conclusion*

This chapter has offered some creative ideas in only a few major areas of our lives. The examples are few but they can give you some idea of how structures are changing for the better. My hope is that they will show you how you can think creatively in your life and so contribute to further positive change in our world.

There will always be need for constructive criticism and change in our lives and in our world. The important thing for all of us to remember is that every person on the planet can be involved in this creative process, because we all have minds of unlimited capacity.

I believe that we must confront young and old, East and West, as well as people of all religions and cultures to realize the unlimited capacity of the human mind. If parents and educators alone can instill this reality in the children of this generation, we could see wonderful, positive change in only 20 years!!!

These are exciting times, times of massive change for the better, times for opening the future to new and innovative ways of living and working, times for seeing the planet as a global community where we are all one family!

The astronauts, when they were on the moon, experienced that planet earth has no divisions. It is a single entity as we are one humanity. We and the planet are one, bound together by the universal energy of love, and destined to live in peace.

When more and more individuals in our world take up this thought, the dream of a peaceful world will become a reality. Consider how the peace process incubated in the minds of millions of people when the Berlin Wall was up. When the thought process was large enough and powerful enough, the government of Russia collapsed and the wall came down. Now we can direct our common effort to building a new and better world, based on unity and creative diversity. Just imagine what we can do when all nations think together on how we can live in peace and how together we can create prosperity for everyone!!! If we, together, can imagine this goal, it will happen!!!

5. Suggested Activities for Chapter VI

1. Who are the people God has given you to love? Go out of your way for one of these people today. Do something to them, or for them, so that they feel your love.

2. Do you have a support group of some kind? A group of friends or family who can help you in your personal growth and development? If not, think about finding such a group, or creating one yourself; perhaps a book club, a prayer group, a Bible study group, a theatre group, etc. (*See Appendix 2 for guidelines to create an Energy Circle*).

3. If you have a business, look up the website for Servant Leadership (www.greenleaf.org) and consider how you can improve your business structure using the ideals of Greenleaf.

4. What can you do to bring servant-leadership ideas into local schools or into your church structures?

5. What can you change in your diet to live a healthier life style? What kind of exercise are you doing, or can you do, on a daily basis to become healthier?

6. Pick up the book, "Biology of Belief" by Bruce Lipton, and learn how your thought process can help you become healthier.

7. Read Masaru Emoto's book "The True Power of Water" and discover how your thought process can help you stay healthy.

8. Get a copy of the movie "What the Bleep Do We Know." Watch it with friends and/or family and then have a discussion.

9. If you are connected in any way with educational institutions, check out the Jefferson Center for Character Education (www.jeffersoncenter.org) and share the information with administration and staff.

10. Make time to see the film "An Inconvenient Truth" by Al Gore and look at the website www.climatecricis.net

EPILOGUE

In these pages we have given you basic but important formation. However, knowledge is only the beginning. If you want true understanding of meditation, you must add personal experience. For that reason we have suggested specific activities at the end of each chapter but these exercises are limited. A total experience can only be achieved through a basic Silva Meditation week-end workshop. If you are serious about a complete understanding of meditation, look into the website www.thesilvamethod.com for a place near you where classes are available.

Your mind is your greatest asset. It is an unlimited potential!!! Learn to use it fully so that you can choose appropriate goals for yourself, develop positive attitudes, and create a full and satisfying life. You and you alone carry the responsibility for doing something with the information that is presented in this book.

Take the time and effort to develop habits of creative thinking, and **I promise you will develop a life filled with love, joy, peace, health, happiness and every other good thing!**

APPENDIX 1

An Ode to Junk

Many many years ago
    When I was just a child
        My life seemed oh so easy
            And living such a joy.

There seemed to be no clutter
    As the days went sailing by;
        "Things" were there for me to use
            They didn't pull me down

Then there came the time to grow
    And move out on my own.
        Things became important now
            But I was not surprised.

I remember things like shoes
    And coats and rings and mugs;
        But little did I understand
            These "things" are awful traps.

Someone made a box for me
    With tender loving care.
        It must have been some 20 years
            And now I ask "From whom?"

Things and things and things and more
    And soon it's all just junk.
        Maybe we should clean it up
            And send it to the dump!

Do you know those friends of yours
    Who save those plastic "things"?

They want to use them later on
But later never comes.

Instead the plastic "things" begin
To grow beyond all dreams.
Now they have a drawer that's full
And making room for more!

Perhaps you too have sacks and bags
You'll use them all some day,
But "I haven't time to clean, my dear"
So pile them up some more!

Books are "things" that help us grow
Especially when we're young
But you don't need to save each one,
It's all inside you now!

How many things you gathered home
From France and Spain and fleas.
"What a chore to dust my house
I'll need a maid, oh please!!!!"

And clothes we save, they just might fit
Someone, someday, somehow
But now you're stuck without much space
"Oh God, send help and quick!"

This all might sound like fun and games
But there's a truth below
"You should be in charge of 'things'
Not 'things' controlling you!"

Are you tied down to things you have
Or are you free to share?
Objects ought to richen life
And not just strip you bare.

You say that friend and spouse come first
  And other people too,
    Until a 'thing' you love gets broke
    And you become unglued.

We often let our anger flare
  Because of foolish "things".
    The truth is "Matter fades;
      Love and friends do not!"

The world in which we live today
  Will tie you down a slave
    If you become attached to foolish "things"
    And waste your life away.

When you must take the journey home
  Your "things" will stay behind,
    Perhaps to cause some hate and pain
    Among your kin and kind!

May I suggest you take some time
  To look around your space,
    Remove the clutter, junk and trash
    And know a life that's free.

There's nothing wrong with using "things"
  It's what God had in mind.
    But maybe "things" have gotten hold
    "Horrors, junkiecide!"

APPENDIX 2

Energy Circle

Some of you may be looking for a more structured approach in a formal support group. Here is an outline for a weekly or monthly group meeting.

One hour meetings are most effective. When the leadership is well prepared to lead, a great deal can be accomplished in a short time. We suggest that you indicate the time to begin and the time to end. Discipline is an important part of Full Thinking and therefore should be reflected in the meeting. Monthly meetings, especially if the group is larger than ten members, can extend to one hour and a half if necessary. However, weekly meetings are ideal. In this case, effective meetings can be accomplished in less than an hour.

When meetings are weekly, we suggest there be a "committee" of four or five people who are willing to share the leadership. With this kind of arrangement, each person can be responsible for one meeting a month and the fifth person can be used as an emergency substitute.

It is best to have the meeting in a neutral place like a community room, a school, or church instead of a private home. In this kind of space, there is less danger of the meeting becoming a purely social gathering.

Food and/or beverages need not be required; they can get in the way of the meeting. However, "tea and crumpets" after the meeting, can allow for more personalized kinds of sharing.

As for the meeting itself, here is a suggested format:

1. Have the group sit in a circle.

2. Begin with one of two minutes of quiet (perhaps with music background) and ask each individual during that time, to recall successes (or blessings) they have experienced since the last meeting.

3. The leader then shares a personal success story – a goal already achieved or some movement toward a goal, or a positive experience at home or work, etc. The leader then invites the person on the right or left to continue around the circle (individuals who do not want to share may simply say, "I Pass").

4. If the group is studying a book:
   a. Have each person read one chapter before the meeting.

   b. Suggest that everyone, as they read, mark passages in the book with which they strongly agree or disagree. Questions can be written in the margins.

   c. Ask for practical applications of the material.

   d. Personal sharing, especially in terms of application, is always valuable. Sometimes the discussion may move away from the subject matter of the book to something important to the individual or the group. Allow for this kind of eventuality.

   e. Do not allow anyone to dominate the group or to use the meeting to bring up personal problems one after another.

5. Allow time for announcements about lectures in the area, TV presentations, books, movies, workshops, etc.

6. Close with a group meditation (either recorded or guided by one of the group)

7. In our "energy circles" no one is allowed to leave until they have shared at least three hugs!

REFERENCE MATERIALS

Belitz, OFM, Justin – "Success: Full Living"– FrJustin-Hermitage.org
Chopra, MD, Deepak – "Quantum Healing"&"How to Know God"
De Chardin, Teilhard – "Phenomenon of Man"
Dharma Singh Khalsa, MD – "Brain Longevity"- www.brain-longevity.com
Dyer, Dr. Wayne – "Getting in the Gap"&"The Power of Intention"
Elgin, Duane – "Voluntary Simplicity"
Ferguson, Marilyn – "Aquarian Conspiracy"
Films – *Take the Lead, Mad Hot Ballroom, The Hobart Shakespeareans 2005, What the Bleep Do We Know, An Inconvenient Truth*
Furst, Dr. Bruno – "You Can Remember"
Gatto, John Taylor – "Dumbing Us Down"
Gore, Al - www.climatecrisis.net
Greenleaf, Robert K – "Servant Leadership"– www.greenleaf.org
Hay, Louise – "You Can Heal Your Life"
Health and Healing – Electro-acupressure, Star Tech Health Services, 801-229-2500 or www.startechhealth.com (to find a certified professional in your area) - Wellness Pro®, Electro Medical Technologies®, 765-592-2192 (Eyelyn Easson)
Institute of Noetic Science (IONS) – www.noetic.org
Jefferson Center for Character Education – www.jeffersoncenter.org
Lipton, PhD, Bruce – "Biology of Belief"
Maloney, George, SJ – "Inward Stillness"
Maltz, Maxwell – "Psycho-Cybernetics"
Mitchell, Capt. Edgar – Institute of Noetic Science (IONS) - www.noetic.org
Monroe Institute – Accelerating the evolution of human consciousness – www.monroeinstitute.org
Mulholland, James and Philip Gulley – "If Grace Is True"
Noorha Foundation – www.aramaiclight.org
Science & Theology News – www.stnews.org
Siegel, MD, Bernie – "Love, Medicine and Miracles"
Silva, Jose – "The Silva Method"
Simonton, O. Carl and Stephanie – "Getting Well Again"
Spong, John Shelby – "Why Christianity Must Change or Die"and "A New Christianity for a New World"
Suzuki, Shunryu – "Zen Mind, Beginner's Mind"

Albums & Books

Title	Price
Success: Full Living: A Mini-Retreat on 3 CDs (**Album**) by Fr. Justin Belitz, OFM	$30.00
Success: Full Living: A Contemporary Approach to Responsible Spirituality (**Book**) by Fr. Justin Belitz, OFM	$15.00
Success: Full Thinking: Tapping into the Unlimited Resources of Mind (**Book**) by Fr. Justin Belitz, OFM	$15.00

Compact Discs

OPUS	Title	Price
OPUS I	**Vol. 1 - A Universal Morning & Evening Meditation -** A set of two meditations; one for morning and one for evening. The image of light is used to represent God and it is specifically created for people of any faith **Vol. 7 – Basic Relaxation -** This CD is specifically designed for people who are beginning meditation or who have trouble relaxing.	$15.00
OPUS II	**Vol. 2 - A Christian Morning & Evening Meditation** A set of two meditations; one for morning and another for evening. The image of Jesus is used in this CD so that it can be used by any Christian. **Vol. 3 - Contemplative Prayer -** A set of two meditations; one for morning and another for evening. It is an example of passive meditation that can be used by persons of any faith.	$15.00
OPUS III	**Vol. 4 - Creating & Maintaining Ideal Weight** This CD is designed to help anyone reach ideal weight. **Vol. 16 - Controlling the Smoking Habit - by Therese Coddington** A meditation for those wishing to be non-smokers.	$15.00
OPUS IV	**Vol. 5 - Healing Relationships -** This CD will assist the meditator in developing a positive attitude toward anyone, especially people who are difficult to be with or to work with. One track is designed to guide a single person and the other is designed for a group. **Vol. 10 - Positive Self-Image -** The purpose of this CD is to help the meditator improve self-image. One track explains how mind and brain create self-image. Another track has a meditation based on several positive affirmations designed to improve anyone's self image.	$15.00
OPUS V	**Vol. 6 - Healing Self -** A meditation for anyone who is ill, either physically, mentally, emotionally, psychologically, or spiritually. **Vol. 9 - Healing Others -** This CD is designed for family and/or friends of the patient. It is a companion to Vol. 6.	$15.00
OPUS VI	**Vol. 8 - The Lords Prayer and the Prayer of St. Francis -** The meditations on tracks 1 and 2 are examples of how a person can base a meditation on any given text. **Vol. 14 - Peace -**This meditation is designed to help the meditator develop a cosmic dimension of peace. Track 3 is for an individual and track 4 is for a group.	$15.00

OPUS VII	**Vol. 13 - Children's Meditation - by Daniel McRoberts** This CD is especially designed for children, but can also be used by adults. Track 1 is for meditation and track 2 is to assist the meditator achieve sleep. The voice is a 13 year old boy. **Vol. 18 Angels Among Us -** Track 3 of this unique recording offers an explanation of angels as God's messengers. Track 4 is a guided meditation to help you connect with <u>your</u> "angels" when working through challenges, difficulties or planning your future.	$15.00
OPUS VIII	**Vol. 11 - My Friend the Sea -** Poetry is meditation! This recording has selections that reflect some beautiful moments in the life of Fr. Justin. It is hoped that your listening will motivate you to write your own poetry. **Vol. 12 - The 23rd Psalm & St. Francis Canticle of Praise -** Tracks 3 and 4 are examples of how meditation can be used with any familiar text, scripture, poem, or prayer.	$15.00
OPUS IX	**Vol. 15 - Music for Meditation - Flutist: Sr. Barbara Piller, OSF / Harpist: Mary Wild** A recording of music appropriate for meditation. Track 1 is flute only and track 2 is harp only. **Vol. 17- Music for Meditation - Clarinet: Rob Carroll / Synthesizer: Andy Consentino -** Track 1 is clarinet only and track 2 is synthesizer only.	$15.00
OPUS X	**Vol. 19 - Learning (made fast and easy)- for students -** This CD is specifically for students, to show them how to use meditation to learn faster and easier. It contains other suggestions for effective study as well. **Vol. 20 - Teaching (made efficient and effective) - for teachers -** This CD is for teachers who wish to be more efficient and effective in the classroom. It deals specifically with relaxation, visualization and other tools to enhance learning.	$15.00

WEAR WHITE ON WEDNESDAYS FOR PEACE

In November of 2007, Fr. Justin presented a workshop in Australia titled: You Can Make A Difference. Scott Shelley, a participant in this workshop, decided to start a worldwide movement for peace. His card reads: "Where ever you're going or what ever you are doing, you are invited to wear white every Wednesday for world peace." The Hermitage is supporting this **effort by** providing T-shirts with this message on the back: "Wear White Every Wednesday for World Peace". On the front of the T-shirt is the logo of the Hermitage and a picture of the Dove of Peace. The T-shirts come in size large and extra-large. The cost of the T-shirt is $15, shipping and handling is $3.

Please help us bring peace to this planet!!!!

French translations available* for Friar Justin Belitz books

*Success: Full Living**
Succès : dites oui !

Les pouvoirs de la visualization
et de la pensée positive

ISBN 2-88353-100-5
© Editions Jouvence, 1996

Success: Full Thinking

Les pouvoirs illimités de l'esprit

ISBN 978-2-88353-658-6
© Editions Jouvence, 1996

French edition of SFL & SFT can be obtained from:

Marietta Kovacs
Work 011-41-22-349-8077
Mobile 011-41-79-342-9977
Fax 011-41-22-349-0184
Work Address: C.P. 276 Chene-Bouorg/Geneva, Switzerland

* *Success: Full Living* is also available in Greek, Hungarian and Polish!

HERMITAGE ORDER FORM

Qty.		Price	Total
	Compact Discs		
	Opus I	$15.00	$
	Opus II	$15.00	$
	Opus III	$15.00	$
	Opus IV	$15.00	$
	Opus V	$15.00	$
	Opus VI	$15.00	$
	Opus VII	$15.00	$
	Opus VIII	$15.00	$
	Opus IX	$15.00	$
	Opus X	$15.00	$
	Album & Books		
	Success: Full Living (Album)	$30.00	$
	Success: Full Living (Book)	$15.00	$
	Success: Full Thinking (Book)	$15.00	$
	T-Shirt — L — XL	$15.00	$
	Donation	$	$
	Shipping & Handling - $3 for 1st item *($1 for each additional)*		$
	Total	$	$

Name			
Address			
Address			
City		State	Zip
Phone	Day ( ) -		ext.
Phone	Eve. ( ) -		ext.

Circle one: **Check**   **Money Order**   **Credit Card**

Circle one: **Visa**   **Master Card**

CC #: _____   Exp.: ___ / ___ / ___   Code: _____

Order online at www.FrJustin-Hermitage.org or fill out this form
and include credit card info, check or money order made out to:

"Franciscan Hermitage"
P. O. Box 30248 Indianapolis, IN 46230
(317) 545-0742
e-mail: frjustin@frjustin-hermitage.org
website: www.FrJustin-Hermitage.org

Lightning Source UK Ltd.
Milton Keynes UK
05 December 2009

147110UK00001B/6/P